Mutiny: The History and Legacy of the Mutinies aboard the
HMS Bounty, the Amistad, and the Battleship Potemkin

By Charles River Editors

The *Potemkin* at sea in 1905

About Charles River Editors

Charles River Editors is a boutique digital publishing company, specializing in bringing history back to life with educational and engaging books on a wide range of topics. Keep up to date with our new and free offerings with this 5 second sign up on our weekly mailing list, and visit Our Kindle Author Page to see other recently published Kindle titles.

We make these books for you and always want to know our readers' opinions, so we encourage you to leave reviews and look forward to publishing new and exciting titles each week.

Introduction

HMS *Wager*

An 18th century depiction of the wreck

"Whereas upon a General Consultation, it has been agreed to go from this Place through the Streights of Magellan, for the coast of Brazil, in our way for England: We do, notwithstanding, find the People separating into Parties, which must consequently end in the Destruction of the whole Body; and as also there have been great robberies committed on the Stores and every Thing is now at a Stand; therefore, to prevent all future Frauds and Animosoties, we are unanimously agreed to proceed as above-mentioned." – John Bulkley, gunner on the HMS

Wager

"I cannot suppose the Captain will refuse the signing of it; but he is so self-willed, the best step we can take, is to put him under arrest for the killing of Mr. Cozens. In this case I will, with your approbation, assume command. Then our affairs will be concluded to the satisfaction of the whole company, without being any longer liable to the obstruction they now meet from the Captain's perverseness and chicanery." – Lieutenant Robert Baynes, second-in-command on the HMS *Wager*

Mention the 18th century Royal Navy and visions come to mind of swashbuckling sailors swinging from rope to rope while a red-faced captain in an even redder coat and a powdered wig shouts order and pitches fits. Such visions, largely shaped by Hollywood pictures such as the popular *Pirates of the Caribbean* franchise, naturally fail to do full justice to a group of men who functioned, with little direction and even less support, on the seas for years at a time. Disney may enjoy portraying them sitting down to sumptuous feasts or cavorting with scantily clad native girls, but the opposite was true; the men were almost always hungry, with even the best meals consisting of little more than bread, beans, and a bit of meat on the side if the voyage was still in its early days. Likewise, those stranded on islands were not met by pretty native girls bearing coconut cream pies but instead cold and wind and an unremitting surf that drove away both flora and fauna.

Those who doubt this reality or unfamiliar with it need only consult the journals and records of the officers and crew of the HMS *Wager*, who sailed from England to fight the Spanish in 1741 and instead ended up fighting for their lives. These men, many of whom were already long past the normal age of service, endured short rations and rough seas for months, only to end up shipwrecked on an island off of South America. Many died during the wreck, as did many others who were marooned, only to discover it bare of almost all supplies necessary for survival. On top of those tribulations, mutinous men rose up violently against their captain and made their way across more than 2,000 miles of tossing seas in an open boat. Their trip was characterized not just by hardship and hunger but also by that most dastardly of crimes – betrayal - as their leaders again and again chose their own good over that of their men.

Of the almost 100 men that set out on the *Wager*, only a handful made it home, and even then they returned not together but piecemeal after having been separated by their troubles. When they finally did make their way back to England, they came home not to a hero's welcome but numerous questions and ultimately a court martial. For a number of reasons, ranging from lack of evidence to prosecutorial reluctance, the men were not convicted of any crimes; in fact, most of the survivors went on to have successful careers in the British Navy and other endeavors. However, no rational person could ever claim that they got away unpunished, for surely the sights of friends dying slowly of starvation and dead bodies piled on beaches for carrion to attack were tougher punishments than the Admiralty could ever mete out on them.

HMS *Bounty*

An illustration depicting the Mutiny on the *Bounty*

"On the Twenty Eight of April at day break the Captain and me were surprised by Mr. Christian, Stewart Young Haywood and the Master at Arms, with twenty one people. Christian and the Master at Arms went into Mr. Bligh's Cabin and tied his hands behind him. Two men came into my Cabin, with muskets and Bayonets, told me if I spoke, that I was a dead man and that Mr. Christian had taken the Ship and that they was to put us onshore upon one of the Friendly Isles." – John Fryer, Master on the *Bounty*

The Mutiny on the *Bounty* is one of those great stories in history that most people have heard of but few people know much about. In fact, those who think they know what happened are likely to have formed their opinions from what they saw on a movie screen than what they read in a book. Fortunately, the true story itself is every bit as exciting as anything Hollywood could dream up.

In April 1789, the HMS *Bounty* was conducting operations in the Pacific when about half of the crew put in action a plot to take control of the ship from its captain, William Bligh. Along with Bligh, most of the rest of the crew that remained loyal to him were cast adrift while the

Bounty sailed off. The mutineers sailed to Pitcairn Island, and they scattered on that island and in Tahiti before scuttling the *Bounty* itself, but in the meantime, Bligh and his loyal crew were managing to successfully travel over 3,000 miles and reach the Dutch East Indies. Eventually, Bligh was able to make it back to report the mutiny in 1790, and the Royal Navy sent another ship, the *Pandora*, to go find and arrest the mutineers. The *Pandora* eventually nabbed 14 of the mutineers, but as if all of that wasn't enough, it ran aground against the Great Barrier Reef, resulting in the deaths of 4 mutineers and dozens of crew.

In the end, three of the mutineers were executed, and several were acquitted or pardoned, but the story became such a part of popular lore in Britain that it has been commemorated and depicted in various ways ever since. Of course, the mutiny on the *Bounty* has been made into several films starring Hollywood legends like Marlon Brando, Clark Gable, and Errol Flynn, and those movies often worked off one of the several novels written about the mutiny.

The *Amistad*

A 19th century engraving depicting the revolt on the Amistad

"25,000 slaves were brought into Cuba every year – with the wrongful compliance of, and personal profit by, Spanish officials." – Dr. Richard Madden

"Now, the unfortunate Africans whose case is the subject of the present representation, have been thrown by accidental circumstances into the hands of the authorities of the United States Government whether these persons shall recover the freedom to which they are entitled, or whether they shall be reduced to slavery, in violation of known laws and contracts publicly passed, prohibiting the continuance of the African slave-trade by Spanish subjects." – Henry Stephen Fox, British diplomat

By the early 19th century, several European nations had banned slavery, but while the United States had banned the international slave trade, slavery was still legal in the country itself. As a result, there was still a strong financial motive for merchants and slave traders to attempt to bring slaves to the Western hemisphere, and a lot of profits to be gained from successfully sneaking slaves into the American South and the Caribbean by way of locations like Havana, Cuba.

At the same time, the cruelties of the slave trade often led to desperate attempts by slaves or would-be slaves to avoid the horrific fate that they were either experiencing or about to face. In 1831, Nat Turner's revolt shocked the South and scared plantation owners across the country, while also bringing the issue of slavery to the forefront of the national debate. But just years after Turner's rebellion was quickly put down, the United States was embroiled in another similar controversy as a result of the successful insurrection aboard the *Amistad*, a Spanish schooner that was carrying Africans taken from modern day Sierra Leone and brought across the Atlantic to Cuba.

In 1839, the *Amistad* was loaded in Havana with Africans who had been brought across the ocean to be made slaves, but after the ship left Havana for another location on Cuba, the Africans escaped their shackles, killed the captain, and took over the ship. When they demanded to be taken back to Africa, the ship's crew instead sailed north, and the ship was ultimately captured off the coast of Long Island in New York by the USS *Washington*. All of this resulted in one of the most famous maritime cases in history, and one that affected not just the international slave trade ban but also how jurisdiction over such a case was determined. While the British were interested in enforcing the ban on the slave trade, Spain wanted to protect its own rights by asserting that their property (crew and ship) could not be subjected to American jurisdiction, and that since slavery was legal in Cuba, a foreign country had no right to determine the legal status of the Africans aboard the *Amistad*. On top of that, both the Spanish slave traders intending to sail the ship around Cuba and the American captain who seized the *Amistad* claimed ownership of the Africans.

The legal case proceeded all the way up to the United States Supreme Court, which eventually affirmed a lower court ruling that allowed the Africans to be returned home as free men, but not before the British and Spanish used diplomatic and political leverage to try to influence the outcome. Ultimately, the rebellion on the *Amistad* and the case that followed became a watershed moment in the debate over slavery and abolition in America about 20 years before the Civil War.

The *Potemkin*

A propaganda poster for the 1925 film about the ship's mutiny

"The hero is the sailors' battleship, the Odessa crowd, but characteristic figures are snatched here and there from the crowd. For a moment, like a conjuring trick, they attract all the sympathies of the audience: like the sailor Vakulinchuk, like the young woman and child on the Odessa Steps, but they emerge only to dissolve once more into the mass. This signifies: no film stars but a film of real-life types." –Adrian Piotrovsky, writing for the Leningrad newspaper *Krasnaia gazeta*

Russia entered the 20th century in possession of nearly all of the prerequisites for an empire of historic proportions. The tsar presided over almost one-sixth of the world's land masses extending from a culturally European West to an Asian East, with vast expanses of forest steppe and tundra reaching from Poland to the Pacific Ocean. Land-based military forces reflected the potency of a globally dominant nation, and the disparate borders offered several strategic advantages for the navy, including Sevastopol in Crimea, and Odessa on the Black Sea. Virtually all great empires have built and maintained advanced navies, from ancient times to the modern era of Spain, but Russia lagged behind in the modern armadas typical of world-shaping societies. This was due, in part, to the enormity of her four major coastlines. To the north stretched a broad icy expanse, thousands of miles in breadth. To the east lay a second vast coastline from the Bering Strait to the south, where it met territory controlled by leading Asian powers. The country possessed sizable inland coasts in the Black Sea requiring a fleet of its own, and a geographically and culturally distinct Baltic region. Many of Russia's major cities were situated far to the interior, St. Petersburg being the exception, and had always enjoyed the natural protection of a wide swath of wilderness and climate resistant to invasion. That fact notwithstanding, an up-to-date naval force was needed in response to exterior threats on frontier borders far from Moscow. Despite a membership of nearly 60,000 sailors by the turn of the 20th century–making Russia's sea-going force the fourth largest in the world–the crews were deficient and poorly treated, drawn largely from conscripted factory workers and serfs who earned far less in wages than they would have at home. This made them particularly susceptible to anti-tsarist ideologies, and in particular, "Marxist agitators." Likewise, most among the officer class were political appointees from the land-based aristocracy, who lacked the general skill and sensitivity with which to lead men into battles they themselves had never experienced.

Despite Russia's imposing image in the world, less apparent weaknesses within the tsarist government threatened the country's stability. The autocratic system had stood firm for several hundred years, but only in the 18th and 19th centuries was it surrounded by emerging democracies, alluring to working classes around the world. Multiple ethnicities from lands conquered in previous centuries maintained an almost provisional membership when faced with the allure of their home empires. Tsar Nicholas II, generally remembered as an ineffective personality with respect to autocratic leadership, was caught between a rigid, older brand of harsh, Russian rule and a surrounding world environment filled with political reform and democracies contrary to Russian political tradition. A believer in the ironclad mode of command bequeathed to him from immediate predecessors, Nicholas was neither firm, knowledgeable, nor charismatic enough to serve as a convincing autocrat. Equally incompetent and weak-willed as a reformer, he responded clumsily and half-heartedly to prevailing sentiments favoring class equality that he could not, in the end, preserve unity among the predominant national factions. What reforms he offered to appease national unrest were all but abandoned once the perceived crisis was over, allowing his return to a comfortable status quo.

As with the rest of the population, naval forces that had come to be persuaded of anti-tsarist arguments did not do so within a vacuum. The accumulated unrest throughout the country could provoke a more organized message within the confines of a single warship, and indeed it eventually resulted in the first far-reaching eruption in the Black Sea Fleet aboard the battleship *Potemkin*. Several events in the early 20th century led to an eroding loyalty among Russian military forces, and *Potemkin* was the first modern ship to reveal it, an act that would bring it fame and make it the subject of some of the most well-known works of film and literature in Russian history.

Mutiny: The History and Legacy of the Mutinies aboard the HMS Wager, the HMS Bounty, the Amistad, and the Battleship Potemkin tells the dramatic stories of these famous mutinies. Along with pictures and a bibliography, you will learn about the mutinies like never before.

Mutiny: The History and Legacy of the Mutinies aboard the HMS Wager, the HMS Bounty, the Amistad, and the Battleship Potemkin

About Charles River Editors

Introduction

HMS *Wager*

  Chapter 1: A Harrowing Voyage

  Chapter 2: A Harrowing Shipwreck

  Chapter 3: A Harrowing Mutiny

  Chapter 4: The Mutineers' Journey Home

  Chapter 5: The Return of Captain Cheap's Group

  Chapter 6: Court Martials and the Aftermath

HMS *Bounty*

  Chapter 1: His Majesty's Armed Vessel the *Bounty*

  Chapter 2: He Frequently Threatened Them

  Chapter 3: Mr. Christian Had Taken the Ship

  Chapter 4: A Most Distressed Situation

  Chapter 5: Rescue the Ship

  Chapter 6: God Knows Whither

  Chapter 7: Everything We Had Saved

  Chapter 8: Shall Suffer Death

The *Amistad*

  Chapter 1: The Amistad's Journey

  Chapter 2: Under What Authority

  Chapter 3: Mutiny and Murder?

  Chapter 4: Unfortunate Under Such Circumstances

  Chapter 5: Supreme Arguments

  Chapter 6: The Ruling

Battleship *Potemkin*

  Unrest and Construction

  The Mutiny

  Odessa

  The End of the Mutiny

  The Legacy of the *Potemkin*

  Online Resources

  Bibliography

Free Books by Charles River Editors

Discounted Books by Charles River Editors

HMS *Wager*

Chapter 1: A Harrowing Voyage

In the 21st century, it can be difficult to comprehend the risks taken by early sailors who set out to sea in ships so small they could comfortably sit on the deck of a modern aircraft carrier or luxury liner. These men sailed for months and sometimes years without being able to contact their families, and often they went nearly as long without setting foot on land. Expeditions in the first few centuries of the Age of Exploration could often find themselves entirely dependent on their wits to survive, as there was little chance of getting outside help if something went wrong.

The ship later known as the *Wager* began her life as an East Indiaman, also known as a "tea clipper," because its main purpose was to carry tea harvested by the East India Company from India to England. Though that sounds like an innocuous duty, it was actually dangerous work, as evidenced by the fact she was armed with nearly 30 guns. She and her crew of around 100 men made several trips back and forth to India between 1735 and 1739, when the British Royal Navy bought her from her owner, a J. Raymond, for use by Commodore George Anson in patrolling the west coast of South America.

Anson

The ship's new owner sent her right on to the Navy shipyard, where through the winter and spring of 1739-40, the Royal Navy spent more than £7,000 fitting her out for naval service. She resumed work on April 22, 1740 as the *Wager*, named not because of any card game but in honor of Admiral Sir Charles Wager, who was sponsoring the voyage. Though well-equipped with guns, the *Wager* was designated a sixth-rate and would be used primarily to carry small weapons and gunpowder, as well as 120 men and 28 guns.

Wager

By this time, Britain was once again at war with Spain, and with that in mind the Duke of Newcastle sent Commodore Anson, with the *Wager* and five other ships, to South America. Newcastle was known to be more of a puppet than a leader, to the extent that historian Harry Dickinson once described him as "notorious for his fussiness and fretfulness, his petty jealousies, his reluctance to accept responsibility for his actions, and his inability to pursue any political objective to his own satisfaction or to the nations profit ... Many modern historians have depicted him as the epitome of unredeemed mediocrity and as a veritable buffoon in office." Therefore, it is quite likely that he was acting at the behest of someone else, perhaps Hubert Tassell or Henry Hutchison, two agents of the South Sea Company who stood to make quite a bit of money if Britain could run the Spanish out of South America. Not only did they sell the Navy supplies for the ships, they also devised a way to join the sailors on their fateful journey, a decision they would undoubtedly come to regret.

Newcastle

Newcastle's ordered Anson "to use your best endeavours to annoy and distress the Spaniards, either at sea or land, to the utmost of your power, by taking, sinking, burning, or otherwise destroying all their ships and vessels that you shall meet with, and particularly their boats, and all embarkations whatsoever, that they may not be able to send any intelligence by sea along the coast of your being in those parts." Furthermore, he told the captain, "In case you shall find it practical to seize, surprise or take any of the towns or places belonging to the Spaniards on the coast, that you may judge worthy of making such an enterprise upon, you are to attempt it; for which purpose we have not only ordered the land forces above mentioned, but have also thought proper to direct that an additional number of small arms be put on board the ships under your command…"

The people that Anson was ordered not to attack were the indigenous peoples, but this was not based on any sense of morality. Newcastle explained that "the number of native Indians on the coast of Chile greatly exceeds that of the Spaniards, and that there is reason to believe that the said Indians may not be averse to join with you against the Spaniards in order to recover their freedom, you are to endeavour to cultivate a good understanding with such Indians as shall be willing to join and assist you in any attempt that you may think proper…"

Writing in 1885, historian John Knox Laughton observed that Anson's mission seems to have been doomed from the start: "The establishment of the navy…and the expense of fitting out the fleet for the West Indies and the coast of Spain swallowed up all the resources of the admiralty. There was thus great difficulty in equipping and manning the ships intended for the Pacific; whilst instead of the regiment of soldiers…a number of pensioners, old, worn-out, and crippled, were put on board, together with a number of newly enlisted and wholly undrilled marines…All this caused great delay, and it was not till 18 September 1740, after eight months' preparation, that the little squadron of six ships put to sea from St. Helens."

It is hard to imagine the physical condition of most of these men, as 18th century people did not retire young to play golf. Those living on their pensions were doing so because they were no longer considered able to work any normal jobs to which they may have been accustomed. Now these men, many of whom were in their 60s and 70s, were being loaded up and sent to endure life aboard leaking, creaking vessels that regularly killed younger, stronger men.

Nevertheless, the king needed warm bodies and no one was exempt; indeed, those too frail to climb the ladder up the side of the ship were hauled up in slings. Anson himself later wrote of these unfortunate men that "the most crazy and infirm only should be culled out for so laborious and perilous an undertaking…whereas the whole detachment that was sent…seemed to be made up of the most decrepit and miserable objects that could be collected out of the whole body; and…these were a second time cleared of that little health and strength which were to be found amongst them…" Perhaps not surprisingly, they proved to be more of a liability than an asset, because it only took a few months before some of them began to die during the voyage, requiring the others to take time out to bury them at sea. Given the various fates that would befall the crew, it is little surprise there are no records of any pensioners aboard the *Wager* making it back home to England.

Regardless, all of these men, along with the younger and healthier sailors, were packed onto the six warships and two transports that set out in August 1740. Weighing in at over 1,000 tons and crewed by 400 men, the *Centurion* was the largest. Then there were the twins, *Gloucester* and *Severn*, both the same size and carrying the same number of men and guns. The *Pearl* was only slightly larger than the *Wager* but carried twice as many men and 40 guns. There was also the little *Tryal*, with a crew of 70 and only eight guns. Sailing along beside the fearsome warships were the *Anna* and *Industry*, carrying additional food and tools for the voyage.

A contemporary painting of the *Centurion* (background) fighting a Spanish ship

When the ships set out on their expedition, none of the British crewmembers were aware that the delays had allowed the French to find out about the expedition and tell the Spanish government. In turn, the Spanish sent its own small flotilla to intercept the men at Madeira. Fortunately for the Spaniards, if not Anson and his men, they had plenty of time to get there, because various troubles plagued the trip enough to delay the British ships' arrival until October 25. However, the British sailors were lucky enough to manage to slip in and out of the port without the Spanish catching them.

As it turned out, that was the first and probably last time fortune smiled on the voyage. Just weeks later, after the *Industry* left to return to England, the warm air began to take its toll on their supplies, and the food started to rot. Moreover, the ships were overcrowded, and while this was a situation that the men normally coped with by spending as much time as possible on deck, the rotting food brought flies, which spread germs throughout the ship and led to an outbreak of typhus. The sick men were subsequently confined to crowded quarters, where the disease spread, bringing with it the scourge of all armies: dysentery.

The crew continued to grow more ill by the day, but finally the ships sighted land just a few days before Christmas and were able to anchor off Santa Catarina Island, along the coast of Brazil. Anson ordered all the sick men ashore, where they were able to recover in fresh air and sunshine, with fresh water and fresh fruit to eat. While they were off the ship, he ordered those remaining behind to scrub down the lower decks and build smoking fires in each compartment to drive out the vermin. He then had men use vinegar to wash down the walls and floors on every level.

Had the ships been able to follow Anson's original plans to get into port, clean up and get out again, all would have gone well. Instead, he ordered all seven ships to remain there for a month while the *Tryal* was repaired. This meant that the men were exposed night and day to malarial mosquito bites, which killed as many men on shore as might have died in the holds of the ship. In fact, when the ships finally left Santa Catarina Island on January 18, 1741, they carried away more sick men than they had brought to shore.

Anson's troubles did not end here, for just a few days later the ships ran into bad weather so severe that it broke the *Tryal*'s newly repaired mast off and crippled the ship. Anson ordered the *Gloucester* to tie off her crippled sister and tow her behind the rest of the party, slowing down everyone's progress. The group also lost the *Pearl*, which drifted off course and away from the flotilla during the storm. Her captain died during the process and was replaced by First Lieutenant Sampson Salt, who was so desperate to find his compatriots that he mistakenly signaled a Spanish flotilla led by José Alfonso Pizarro (not to be confused with conquistador Francisco Pizarro). The *Pearl* managed to escape and reunite with the English ships, but only by throwing everything possible overboard in order to lighten the load.

Pizarro

After stopping briefly for repairs at St. Julian, the British ships sailed on toward Cape Horn, encouraged by improving weather. In March 1741, Anson ordered the *Tryal* to take the lead, charging her crew with spotting any ice that was ahead. Already damaged and poorly repaired, the *Tryal* was no match for the job and had to be replaced by the *Pearl*, leading Captain Saumarez of the *Tryal* to drearily record in his journal that "really life is not worth pursuing at the expense of such hardships."

As if starvation, thirst, dysentery, typhus and storms were not enough, the men also began to feel the effects of scurvy, a dreaded disease that afflicted sailors for centuries. Caused by a lack of Vitamin C, it decimated Anson's men during the weeks they spent trying to round Cape Horn. To make matters worse, the severe storms left even the best navigators in the crew unable to calculate exactly where the ships were in relation to the land.

Thus, it came as a shock when, on the night of April 13, a sailor standing watch on the *Anna* looked across the sea and saw the high cliffs of Cape Noir outlined by the moonlight only a couple of miles away. The *Anna* fired warning shots and waved lanterns just in time to warn the other ships off, and a chaplain aboard the *Centurion* would write of Cape Noir, "It was indeed most wonderful, that the currents should have driven us to the eastward with such strength; for the whole squadron esteemed themselves upwards of ten degrees more westerly than this land, so that in running down, by our account, about nineteen degrees of longitude, we had not really advanced half that distance. And now, instead of having our labours and anxieties relieved by approaching a warmer climate and more tranquil seas, we were to steer again to the southward, and were again to combat those western blasts, which had so often terrified us; and this too, when we were greatly enfeebled by our men falling sick, and dying apace, and when our spirits, dejected by a long continuance at sea, and by our late disappointment, were much less capable of supporting us in the various difficulties, which we could not but expect in this new undertaking."

As fate would have it, the escape from this close call would prove to be only a short respite from danger.

Chapter 2: A Harrowing Shipwreck

On the night of April 23, just 10 days after avoiding near disaster, an even stronger storm hit, and this one managed to scatter the ships and rip the *Wager*'s sails to shreds. In anticipation of such an event possibly occurring, the various ships had been given rendezvous points to meet back up if they got separated, and of the three potential rendezvous points, Anson would end up sailing to the Juan Fernández Islands off the coast of Chile. In addition to the *Wager* being blown off course, the *Severn* and *Pearl* also got separated, and the captains of those ships eventually decided to return across the Atlantic back to England without trying to link back up with Anson.

Meanwhile, the *Wager*'s captain, David Cheap (who had been promoted after Captain Dandy Kidd had died aboard the ship before reaching Cape Horn), had difficulty not only navigating the ship but simply sailing it, thanks to the damage done by the storms and the poor condition of the men on board. With so many disabled by illness, the *Wager* barely had more than a dozen fit men able to operate the ship, and Cheap made the mistake of trying to head for a different rendezvous point than Anson. Ironically, Cheap, despite being mostly confined by his own sickness, overruled suggestions that the *Wager* head for the Juan Fernández Islands.

As it turned out, the *Wager* would not sail far enough west to reach the rendezvous point before the ship was steered north, getting itself lost in a bay the sailors knew nothing about. Captain Cheap later wrote miserably of how the ship was wrecked in the early hours of the morning of May 14 on the rocks around Patagonia. The weather, he said, was foul (in fact, they were in the midst of a hurricane), and the ship had already lost her mizzen-mast, making it nearly impossible to sail in the fierce winds. Most of the soldiers were sick with scurvy or dysentery or both, and everyone was hungry and very thirsty. He was himself in very poor shape, recalling that "on the afternoon before the ship was lost, as I was walking along the deck…to give some directions about repairing of four of the chain-plates…I was thrown down one of the hatchways, and was so unlucky as to dislocate the upper bone of my left arm. I was taken up very much stunned and hurt with the violence of the fall and dislocation, which cost the Surgeon two or three hours of trouble to reduce, and bring me to myself."

Ever mindful of the needs of his men, Cheap sent for his second-in-command, Robert Baynes, and his gunner and warned them about the dire situation. He also gave them orders that he later claimed would have saved the ship, only to be ignored: "But my Lieutenant [Baynes]…went…to his bottle, without giving himself any farther concern about the preservation of His Majesty's ship. The Surgeon, contrary to my knowledge, laid me asleep with an opiate…. So that I knew nothing of what was doing in the ship…till half an hour past four next morning, the time when the ship first struck, although my Lieutenant had orders…to inform me if we had any ground with the lead, and of the winds and weather."

Awakening to find the ship stuck on the rocks, the captain, no doubt still compromised by the opiate he had been given, could do little but remain with his sick crew as the waves pounded the ship. Cheap wrote that he was "expecting the ship every moment to go to pieces." The rudder broke and knocked a hole in the bottom of the ship, flooding the lower levels but not knocking her from the rocks.

When the sun rose, he saw that they were stranded off the coast of the Cordillaras islands. With no other alternative presenting itself, the men decided to try to make their way ashore. Midshipman Alexander Campbell later recalled Cheap's noble reply when he offered to help his injured captain ashore: "His answer was, Go and save all the sick, and don't mind me. He also gave orders for hoisting the boats out as soon as possible…. I observed that this very day, the spirit of discord and dissension had entered the people. When I required some of them to return with me in the yawl, to fetch such things from the ship as were necessary for every man…they plainly answered, that they would not go." Campbell did go back for his captain, assuring him that everyone else who wanted to had already headed for shore. What Campbell did not mention was that, because they were so sick and weak, some of the men never made it but were instead swept away by the waves.

On the other hand, Campbell did report that food was scarce and shelter almost nonexistent. Campbell would write, "There was on the island two or three huts built by the Indians…. One of these was fixed on for the Captain; and happy for him it was, that any habitation could be had: for in his condition he had certainly lost his life without such a shelter, as many of the people afterwards did. As soon as the Captain got into this hut, he ordered me to take the yawl, and see if the men on board would come ashore."

Unfortunately, it seems that Cheap's concern for his crew was, perhaps, too little too late, for when Campbell arrived back at the ship, he "found them all in such confusion as cannot be imagined." The men had helped themselves to the ship's weapons and liquor, and they were completely intoxicated. Campbell explained, "Some were singing psalms, others fighting, others swearing, and some lay drunk on the deck. ...[O]bserving some casks of ball and powder on the quarterdeck, I began to put them into the boat; whereupon two of the men came to me, crying out, 'Damn ye! You shall not have them, for the ship is lost and it is ours.' A third came with a bayonet, swearing he would kill me; ...he threw the bayonet at me...I immediately...returned to the shore."

A number of these men perished on the ship itself, their minds likely broken by the effects of scurvy and unlimited alcohol. Among the handful of sailors who survived on the vessel was one John King, who soon put himself forth as their leader. As historian Alan Gurney observed, "The first thing that strikes one when reading the narratives is the complete and utter breakdown of authority aboard the Wager. Suddenly, at a stroke, the strict hierarchical discipline of the Royal Navy tumbles into total anarchy. The scenes aboard the grounded vessel, her masts cut down and her hull pounded by waves, are ones straight out of the Grand Guignol. Men break into the weapon chests and arm themselves with swords, muskets and pistols...Brandy and wine barrels are broached and drunks reel around the deck, some to fall down hatches and then drown in the flooded bilge. Some men sing Psalms, other fight. One man is murdered, strangled to death. This bacchanalia becomes Surrealist when men break open the merchandise chests containing clothing, and then parade the deck wearing velvet coats, laces and ribbons over their soiled canvas trousers and shirts."

Chapter 3: A Harrowing Mutiny

Perhaps it was just as well that the men had a few last laughs, because most of the 140 men who did reach land would not live for long as the weather and other conditions drained the last life out of their already fragile bodies. One of the men who did survive the ordeal, a Mr. Jones, later recalled, "Whichever way we looked a scene of horror presented itself. On one side the wreck (in which was all we had in the world to support and subsist us), together with a boisterous sea, presented us with the most dreary prospect; on the other, the land did not wear a much more favourable appearance: desolate and barren, without sign of culture, we could hope to receive little other benefit from it than the preservation it afforded us from the sea. It must be confessed this was a great and merciful deliverance from immediate destruction; but then we had wet, cold, and hunger to struggle with, and no visible remedy against any of these evils. Exerting ourselves, however, though faint, benumbed, and almost helpless, to find some wretched covert against the extreme inclemency of the weather, we discovered an Indian hut at a small distance from the beach within a wood, in which as many as possible without distinction crowded themselves..." Fittingly, the men had found themselves stranded on what was soon to be known as Wager Island.

Even this shelter would prove to be but poor comfort, as Jones also noted that "here our situation was such as to exclude all rest and refreshment by sleep from most of us; for besides that we pressed upon one another extremely, we were not without our alarms and apprehensions of being attacked by the Indians, from a discovery we made of some of their lances and other arms in our hut; and our uncertainty of their strength and disposition gave alarm to our imagination, and kept us in continual anxiety."

Those who were strong enough to do so built simple shelters out of cloth that the ship had carried to trade with the native peoples, and while the living found precious little to eat, there was plenty of rum rescued from the ship's stores to drink. Soon, they were spending more and more time numbed to their surroundings by the comfort and false warmth the alcohol provided, and before long, many joined their other fallen comrades.

Perhaps inevitably, the breakdown in cohesion and the anger many survivors harbored toward Cheap for the wreck set the stage for a mutiny. Order broke down entirely, and men began to fight to the death over the most meager rations. King added to the tension by insisting that those who had reached shore should risk their lives to return to the ship and pick him and those who were still alive up. When Cheap failed to move fast enough to suit him, he fired on the captain's hut, putting a four pound cannonball through the top of it.

Tragically, the men might have been rescued right away had the weather not been so bad as to prevent them for seeing the *Anna*, which traveled near them along this time. As Anson later put it, "I cannot but observe how much it is to be lamented that the *Wager*'s people had no knowledge of her being so near them on the coast; for as she was not above thirty leagues distant from them, and came into their neighbourhood about the same time the *Wager* was lost, and was a fine roomy ship, she could easily have taken them all on board, and have carried them to Juan Fernandes." He added sorrowfully, "Indeed, I suspect she was still nearer to them than what is here estimated; for several of the *Wager*'s people, at different times, heard the report of a cannon, which I conceive could be no other than the evening gun fired from the Anna pink, especially as what was heard at Wager's Island was about the same time of the day."

Meanwhile, Cheap, still recovering from his wounds, believed that they must travel north if they had any hope of rejoining the other English ships. Most of the men disagreed, wanting to instead travel south in hopes of finding a more hospitable island on which to recover. The men who disagreed were led by gunner John Bulkley. He suggested that if the ship's carpenter, John Cummins, could enlarge the longboat, it might be converted to a schooner. Along with the cutter and the barge, this might allow the men to sail for the Strait of Magellan and from there, home. Cheap considered his proposal for a time but ultimately turned it down, insisting that the men had a duty to try to find Anson and complete their mission. If he failed to do so, or at least to try, he could himself be charged with dereliction of duty, or even worse, cowardice, a capital offense.

Although his own warrant officers spoke out on behalf of Bulkley's plan, Cheap remained resolute, exhibiting a determination that ultimately led to mutiny. Of course, mutiny was also a capital offense unless the mutineers could later justify their decisions before a military court, so the men began to put together a case for their actions even as they planned them.

Their first justification for what they were doing was based on a fear of personal safety claim after an incident involving Captain Cheap shooting an intoxicated crewmember in early June. Had Cheap allowed the man to sober up and then flogged him, no one would have thought much of it, but no captain, even in the most dire straits, could reasonably be expected to pull out his pistol and shoot a man in the face. Midshipman John Byron, whose personal memoirs still remain one of the most popular accounts of the *Wager*'s travails, described the incident in defense of the part he played in the mutiny: "Mr. Cozens was at the store-tent; and having, it seems, lately had a quarrel with the Purser, and now some words arising between them, the latter told him he was come to mutiny; and without any further ceremony fired a pistol at his head, which narrowly missed him. The Captain, hearing the report of the pistol, and perhaps the Purser's words that Cozens was come to mutiny, ran out of his hut with a cocked pistol, and without asking any questions immediately shot him through the head."

Naturally, everyone, including Byron, came running to see what the gunfire meant. Byron continued, "[What] I saw was Mr. Cozens on the ground weltering in his blood. He was sensible, and took me by the hand, as he did several others, shaking his head as if he meant to take leave of us." Appalled by what he witnessed that day, Byron wrote, "If Mr. Cozens' behaviour to the Captain was indecent and provoking, the Captain's on the other hand was rash and hasty. If the first was wanting in that respect and observance which is due from a petty officer to his commander, the latter was still more ill advised in the method he took for the enforcement of his authority, of which indeed he was jealous to the last degree, and which he saw daily declining and ready to be trampled upon."

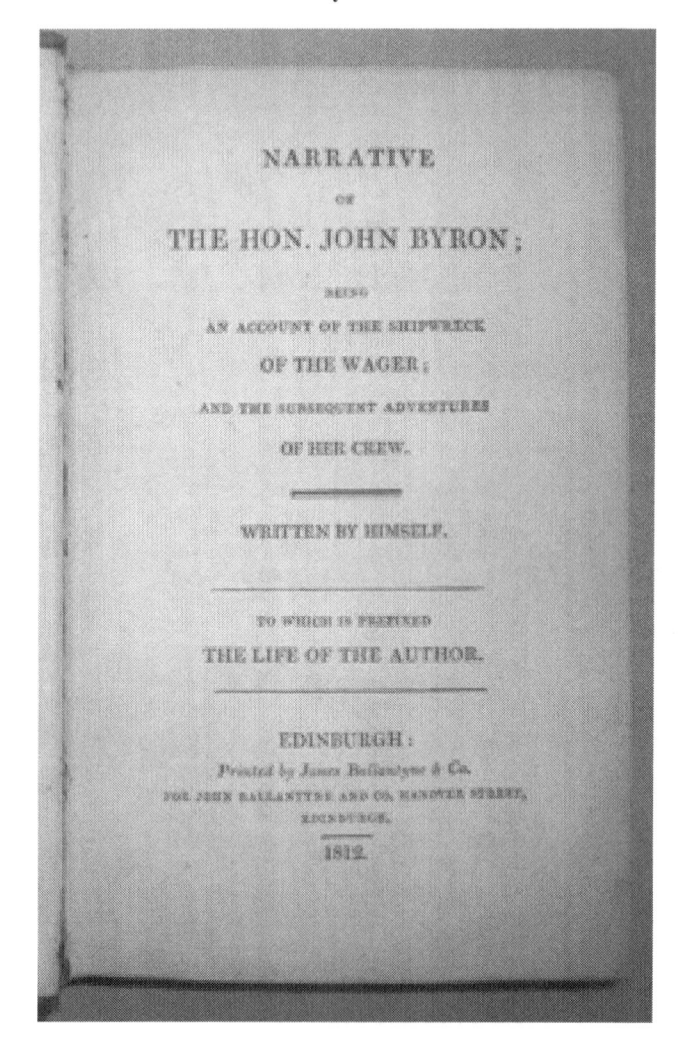

The cover page of an edition of Byron's memoirs

To make matters worse, the man in question, Cozens, did not die right away but instead lingered for 10 days. Cooper, whose account was at least somewhat sympathetic to the captain, nonetheless recorded, "After the extraction of the ball the wound dressed kindly, and there was a likelihood of his recovering. Hereupon he expressed an inclination of being moved to the tent where he had lodged before this mischief befell him. The Gunner and Carpenter, whose tent that was, not presuming to act in this matter without the Captain's permission, waited on him for that purpose, earnestly praying him to indulge the sick man's desire."

Here was a chance for Cheap to show some remorse for his hasty action, but Cooper could only report, "But so far was he from condescending to what they most reasonably asked, that he vehemently replied, 'No. The scoundrel shan't be gratified.' ... The people propagated the disaffection from one to another in their cabals, muttering it would be more honourable of him to dispatch the prisoner at once than force him thus to languish out his miserable hours in a doleful cold wet place, dying as it were by piecemeal."

In reference to Cheap's apparent cruelty, Cooper could only say that "the Captain's austerity, in respect of Cozens, might not proceed from inhumanity or mere resentment...but from an apprehension of its being fitting at that time and in those circumstances to behave with intrepid steadiness, and to betray no symptom of irresolution or weakness. On Wednesday the 24th instant this unfortunate contentious fellow expired, after lingering fourteen days from the time of his being wounded. His shipmates buried him with all the decent formality their situation would then admit of."

Pointing to the Cozens incident as the turning point that ensured the subsequent mutiny, Byron concluded, "[Cheap's] mistaken apprehension of a mutinous design in Mr. Cozens, the sole motive of his rash action, was so far from answering the end he proposed by it, that the men, who before were much dissatisfied and uneasy, were by this unfortunate step thrown almost into open sedition and revolt. It was evident that the people...were extremely affected with this catastrophe of Mr. Cozens.... Their minds were now exasperated, and...their resentment...would shortly show itself in some desperate enterprise."

By the time Cozens was dead and the schooner was completed, a confrontation was inevitable. It came when Bulkley presented Cheap with a document that read as a clear ultimatum: "Whereas upon a General Consultation, it has been agreed to go from this Place through the Streights of Magellan, for the coast of Brazil, in our way for England: We do, notwithstanding, find the People separating into Parties, which must consequently end in the Destruction of the whole Body; and as also there have been great robberies committed on the Stores and every Thing is now at a Stand; therefore, to prevent all future Frauds and Animosoties, we are unanimously agreed to proceed as above-mentioned."

When he read the letter, Lieutenant Baynes, who had previously been loyal to Cheap, surprised the men by saying, "I cannot suppose the Captain will refuse the signing of it; but he is so self-willed, the best step we can take, is to put him under arrest for the killing of Mr. Cozens. In this case I will, with your approbation, assume command. Then our affairs will be concluded to the satisfaction of the whole company, without being any longer liable to the obstruction they now meet from the Captain's perverseness and chicanery."

The mutineers took Bayne's words as a suggestion. According to Bulkley, "Friday the 9th, this morning went in a body and surprised the Captain in bed, disarmed him, and took everything out of his tent. ...The Captain said, gentlemen, do you know what you have done, or are about? He was answered, yes, sir; our assistance was demanded by Captain Pemberton, to secure you as a prisoner for the death of Mr. Cozens; and as we are subjects of Great Britain, we are obliged to take you as such to England."

If Bulkley's account was accurate, it appears Cheap was more than willing to give his men the benefit of the doubt and believe that they were more mistaken than truly mutinous. Either way, Bulkley continued, "The Captain said, gentlemen, Captain Pemberton has nothing to do with me; I am your commander still; I will show you my instructions; which he did to the people. On this we came out. ... I could not think you would serve me so. It was told him, sir, it is your own fault; you have given yourself no manner of concern for the public good…but have acted quite the reverse…as if we had no commander…"

Had they stopped there, the men might never have been charged with mutiny, but they took further steps, including locking up Marine Lieutenant Hamilton. Though taken aback, Cheap maintained his wits enough to quip, "Well 'Captain' Baynes! You will doubtless be called to account for this hereafter."

Chapter 4: The Mutineers' Journey Home

In the wake of the mutiny, 81 men left the island on October 13, 1741, 5 months after being shipwrecked, in the schooner they called *Speedwell*. Bulkley tried to get Cheap to go with them, but the captain refused, and the leader of the mutineers was more than happy to leave him behind to suffer what he felt sure was an imminent death. However, The *Dublin Gazette* later quoted Bulkley as claiming, "Provision deliver'd to the captain, surgeon, and lieutenant Hamilton, with eight deserters, which last are to be at half allowance of the-quantity made out to the people: which make the whole number seven at whole allowance. To the captain, surgeon, and lieutenant Hamilton, six pieces of beef, six pieces of pork, and ninety pound of flour: For the deserters, eight pieces of beef, eight pieces of pork, one hundred weight of flour."

One must indeed marvel at Bulkley's description of those who chose to remain with their captain as "deserters." But an even bigger lie was yet to be told, for the *Gazette* next quoted him as saying, "As soon as the above things were deliver'd we got ready for sailing. I went and took my leave of the captain; he repeated his injunction, That at safe return to England, I would impartially relate all proceedings; he spoke to me in the most tender and affectionate manner, and…desired me to accept of a suit of his best wearing apparel: At parting, he gave me his hand with a great deal of cheerfulness, wishing me well and safe to England."

No man would dare to tell such an obviously false story unless he felt quite certain that no one who knew the truth would live long enough to tell it. In fact, Bulkley made it clear that he believed Cheap to be dead, even as he insisted that he hoped the former captain was alive: "This was the last time I ever saw the unfortunate captain Cheap. However, we hope to see him again in England, that Mr. Cummins and myself maybe freed from some heavy imputations to our prejudice laid on us by the gentleman who succeeded him in command, and who, having an opportunity of arriving-before us in England, not only in the place he touched at abroad, but at home, has blackened us with the greatest calumnies..."

Among them was Midshipman Isaac Morris, who documented the early days of the *Speedwell*'s treacherous voyage: "[W]e put to sea in our longboat and cutter...leaving Capt. Cheap and nineteen others on Wager Island.... Our design was to steer alongshore, through the Straits of Magellan, to the coast of Brazil, which, though a desperate undertaking in such a part of the world, remarkable for tempestuous winds and tumbling seas, we engaged in it with the utmost cheerfulness, being buoyed up with the hopes of once more seeing our native country."

The mutineers seemed to be cursed from the very beginning. Shortly after setting sail, the barge that they took along with them kept splitting its sails, resulting in Bulkley ordering a number of men, including Byron and Campbell, to take it back to Wager Island and hang it with new rigging. According to Cheap, he greeted the men warmly and easily persuaded them to stay behind with him and await rescue, though Campbell, more than a little inclined to paint himself as a hero, told a slightly different tale: "On the 17th, being now out at sea, I had an opportunity of speaking to the people that were with me in the barge, and represented to them, what a shame it was to leave their captain in such a situation; and added, 'That if they did get home, which they could not reasonably hope to do the way they were going, they would be hanged for mutiny; but if, on the other hand, we should go back to the captain, and with him to the northward, we had a much better chance.'"

Campbell continued on by explaining how he just so happened upon the luck needed to make his plan work: "My discourse wrought upon most of them, and they consented to go back; but at the same time objected to our want of provisions, and observed, that it would be dangerous to ask those in the boat for any, lest they should take the barge from us. However...it luckily happened that Mr. Bulkley...ordered me to return with the barge to Wager Island...and to bring off a tent belonging to Captain Pemberton, of the marines, which he said he should want, to make sails for the boat."

Campbell even took credit for taking Byron along, adding, "I observed to the. Hon. Mr. Byron...that now was the time, if he had a mind to go back to the captain. This he immediately resolved to do, but was afraid our new chiefs would suspect our intention, and stop our voyage: but they did not, and we happily got safe to Wager Island that night, where the captain gladly received us."

However it happened, Byron, Campbell, William Harvey, David Buckley, William Ross, Richard Noble, Peter Plastow, Joseph Clinch, Rowland Crusset, and John Bosman all headed back to Wager Island and stayed put. It did not take long for Bulkley to wonder what had become of his men, and since he did not think they had been lost at sea, he decided to return to Wager Island in an effort to find them. By the time Bulkley and the other mutineers arrived, Wager Island had been deserted.

Now down to only two small ships, Bulkley returned to his southward course, but he seemingly failed to take into consideration that a crew made up of mutineers could hardly be counted on to remain loyal to their new captain. Thus, he was caught by surprise on November 3 when the crew of the cutter abandoned the schooner to make their own way. Without the cutter, there was no way for the men to make land and forage for food.

Despairing of survival in the frigid south, the men of the *Speedwell* rallied to some small hope when, just a few days later, the cutter rejoined them, but only days after that, the cutter broke loose in the night and floated quickly to shore, where she wrecked on the rocks. Bulkley, who had judged Cheap so harshly, had lost $1/8^{th}$ of his crew during his first two weeks in command, but he still couldn't feed everyone he still had left, so he marooned 10 other poor men along the southern coast of Chile.

Now with only 60 men left to provide for, Bulkley finally made it to the notorious Strait of Magellan, where he quickly realized that a small crew, while easy to feed, was hard-pressed to successfully navigate the treacherous waters, as everyone remaining had to stand lengthy watches and learn jobs that they had not been trained for in the past. Morris later recalled, "In our passage several of our companions were starved to death, and those of us who survived were so miserably reduced, through want of nourishment, that we had scarce strength to do our duty. … On January the 10th, 1741-42, almost destitute of provisions, we were blessed with the agreeable prospect, distant about seven leagues. …we saw a great many wild horses and some dogs."

These otherwise unappetizing sources of protein looked pretty good to the starving men, and 14 of them thought strong enough to make it to shore set out swimming for the island on January 12, 1742. 13 of them would make it, with one of them proving unable to make it. Morris closed his account of this incident with the following words: "After we had walked about a mile in from the beach, we saw a great number of wild horses and dogs…. There were large flocks of parrots about the rocks, and near the waterside a few seal. We likewise met with a good spring of fresh water…. We shot a wild horse and some seal, and filled three casks with fresh water…. Soon after which the schooner stood farther off at sea, the sea breeze blowing strong."

A few days later, Bulkley sent another 8 men ashore along the coast of Patagonia, ostensibly to gather water, and then left them behind on the island, reducing his crew to 33. After another week or two, 30 starving men finally made it to shore on the southern coast of the Brazil. They had travelled 2,500 miles in the improvised craft and were soon able to arrange passage aboard the *Saint Catherine*, a brigantine that, while far from luxurious, must have seemed so to men who had spent 15 weeks sailing in some of the roughest seas in the world in an open craft. They were welcomed warmly by Portugal's royal governor, a meeting Bulkley recounted in his account: "The Governor…told us we were more welcome to him in the miserable condition we arrived than if we had brought all the wealth in the world with us. …he fully assured us that he would dispatch us the first opportunity to Rio Janeiro; and whenever we stood in need of anything, he ordered us to acquaint the Commandant, and our wants should be instantly supplied. He then took leave of us, and wished us well."

In spite of this warm welcome, the mutineers' troubles were far from over. In short order, the 30 castaways found that they had traded deadly waters for equally dangerous political and bureaucratic red tape. While Bulkley tried to negotiate passage for his men back to England, John King, always the troublemaker, devoted himself to leading a group of disenchanted shipmates in harassing Bulkley and the others, leading them to finally relocate in order to get away from him. According to Captain S.W.C. Pack, "As soon as the ruffians had gone, the terrified occupants left their house via the back wall and fled into the country. Early the next morning they called on the consul and asked for protection. He readily understood that they were all in mortal peril from the mad designs of the boatswain [King] and placed them under protection and undertook to get them on board a ship where they could work their passage."

Finally, on May 20, Bulkley and his followers set sail on the *Saint Tubes* for Bahia and then Lisbon. On October 1, the British Consul there reported, "Last week four officers of the Wager which went out with Mr. Anson…two lieutenants of marines and four sailors arrived here in a Portuguese vessel; they say they were cast away upon an uninhabited island in the South Seas in May last…after they had lost their ship they lengthened their longboat and threw a deck over her in which & two open boats the whole crew being 81 in number resorted to put to sea, except their Captain…" The consul innocently passed on Bulkley's lie that Cheap refused to sail with them because he thought the ship would be unable to make the trip.

The consul also sent back other information about the mutineers' harrowing return to Europe: "One of the boats put back…, the others proceeded, sailed the Straights of Magellan, kept along the coast 'till they got to Rio Grande, where they say they were well received by the Portuguese. But before they got there several of the people died in the voyage…. The rest sailed again from thence and went to Rio de Janeiro, what numbers landed there they do not remember. …Lieutenant [Baynes] says…the sailors were become masters and would not suffer him to keep a journal." The fact Bulkley had intentionally marooned a number of sailors was conveniently omitted.

The consul concluded his report by writing, "When they got to the Rio de Janeiro…lots of their companions who left them at Rio Grande had been there & were gone away in His Majesty's ship commanded by Captain Smith who sailed for the West Indies seven or eight days before they got in. The officers gone home of this Packet [i.e. HMS Stirling Castle] & the sailors are put on board His Majesty's ship the Greyhound."

Once in Spain, the men were able to book passage to England, where they arrived on the first day of 1743. By the time they arrived, Baynes had already started to regret his involvement in the affair and immediately went to the Admiralty so that he might tell his side of the story first. The problem was, of course, that as the senior officer among the mutineers, he automatically bore responsibility for the actions of the men under his command.

Fortunately for Baynes, the Admiralty was not inclined to blacken the name of such a high ranking officer and instead ordered that Bulkley and Cummins be arrested and held on HMS *Stirling Castle* until they could decide whether or not to charge them with any crime. It did not help their cause that they had recently co-authored a book which claimed to be "a faithful Narrative of the Loss of his Majesty's Ship the Wager, on a desolate Island…. With the Proceedings and Conduct of the Officers and Crew and the hardships they endur'd in the said Island for the Space of five Months; their bold Attempt for Liberty, in Coasting the Southern Part of the vast Region of Patagonia; letting out with upwards of eighty Souls in their Boats; the Desertion of the Crew with the Barge; their Passage through the Streights of Magellan…" The book also contained "an Account of their manner of living in the Voyage on Seals, wild Horses, Dogs, &c. and the incredible Hardships they frequently underwent for Want of Food of any Kind; a Description of the several Places where they touch'd in the Streights of Magellan, with an Account of the inhabitants &c. and their safe Arrival to the Brazil, after sailing One Thousand Leagues, in a Long-Boat…." But wait, as the saying goes, there's more, including details related to "their Reception from the Portuguese; an Account of the Disturbances at Rio Grand; their Arrival at Rio Janeiro; their Passage and Usage on Board a Portuguese Ship to Lisbon; and their Voyage to England. Interspers'd with many entertaining and curious Observations, not taken Notice of by Sir John Narborough, or any other Journalist."

Not surprisingly, all of Britain was fascinated by the story. The *Dublin Gazette* published an excerpt describing the natives encountered by the returning crewmen: "The Indians we saw in the Straits of Magellan are people of a middle stature and well-shaped, their complexion of a tawny olive colour, their hair exceeding black, but not very long, they have round faces and small noses, their eyes little and black, their teeth are smooth and even, and close set, of an incomparable whiteness…they are very alive in body, and run with a surprising agility, they wear on their heads white feather a caps, their bodies are cover'd with the skins of seal and guanacos. The women, as soon as they saw us, fled into the woods, so that we can give no description of them." Bulkley and the others would soon enough have a chance to give a more detailed description of the people of the New World, as some of them would prove critical to their chances of being freed.

After considering what to do with Bulkley and Cummins for two weeks, the court decided to release the men pending the arrival back in England of either Anson or Cheap, either of whom, it was assumed, could give a corroborating or conflicting account of events.

Anson made it back to England in 1744, but he was obviously unable to shed any significant light on the events that took place after he lost sight of the *Wager*, so the court decided to wait for Cheap. For Bulkley, this must have seemed to be the end of all his troubles, as he never expected to see his former captain alive again. In fact, he felt so sure of his position that he sold his journal to a local publisher and awaited the accolades he felt would surely follow its release. Even as many believed there was no way to describe his actions as anything other than mutiny, the lack of formal charges against him allowed him to quickly be put in command of the *Saphire*, a privateer ship. The London papers soon began reporting his escapades with relish.

Chapter 5: The Return of Captain Cheap's Group

Much to everyone's surprise, Cheap did make it back home, reaching his native shore on April 9, 1745, and if possible, his group's return was just as perilous and adventurous as Bulkley's group.

After months stranded on Wager Island, Cheap and the others decided to take the two ships they had left, the barge and the yawl, up the South American coast and try to make their way to Chile. They soon lost the yawl to bad weather and faced the dreaded situation of not having enough room for everyone to continue the voyage. Campbell remembered, " "The loss of the yawl was a great misfortune to us who belonged to her (being seven in number) all our clothes, arms, etc. being lost with her. As the barge was not capable of carrying both us and her own company, being in all seventeen men, it was determined to leave four of the Marines on this desolate place. This was a melancholy thing, but necessity compelled us to it. And as we were obliged to leave some behind us, the marines were fixed on, as not being of any service on board. What made the case of these poor men the more deplorable, was the place being destitute of seal, shellfish, or anything they could possibly live upon. The captain left them arms, ammunition, a frying pan, and several other necessaries."

This left 14 men crowded onto the small barge, but the crew still couldn't make any headway and eventually opted to return to Wager Island two months later. Perhaps discouraged by his men's disloyalty or just too tired to keep on trying, Cheap lost all his sense of duty at this point and began to spend his time laying about and fighting with the others over his ration of food.

The men remaining at this point might never have made it home had a group of natives not come to their rescue about two weeks after they had returned to Wager Island. The natives guided the British sailors to a Spanish settlement, but the overland journey took its toll on the already weak men and only four ultimately made it to safety: Marine Lieutenant Hamilton, Campbell, Byron, and Cheap.

The English sailors reached Chaco, but their troubles were still far from over. At that Spanish colonial possession, they were held prisoner by the town's governor for seven months, though their ordeal there was not nearly as bad as it might have been since they were housed with local families and pretty much given the run of the area. In fact, so comfortable were their surroundings that Byron soon found himself with a new problem: he caught the eye of an older woman who was not inclined to let him leave her home. He later wrote, "Whilst we were at Castro, the old lady…sent to the governor, and begged I might be allowed to come to her for a few weeks; this was granted, and accordingly I went and passed about three weeks with her very happily, as she seemed to be as fond of me as if I had been her own son. She was very unwilling to part with me again, but as the governor…sent for me, and I left my benefactress with regret."

It turned out this was far from the end of Byron's lady problems, for he again caught the eye of a young woman, this one said to be the wealthiest heiress on the island. She apparently begged her uncle to set up a match, and Byron reported, "As the old man doted upon her, be readily agreed to it; and accordingly, on the next visit I made him, acquainted me with the young lady's proposal, and his approbation of it, taking me at the same time into a room where there were several chests and boxes, which be unlocked, first shewing me what a number of fine clothes his niece had, and then his own wardrobe, which he said should be mine at his death." While the young sailor held strong against these temptations, one nearly took him in: "Amongst other things, he produced a piece of linen, which he said should immediately be made up into shirts for me. I own this last article was a great temptation to me; however, I had the resolution to withstand it, and made the best excuses I could for not accepting of the honour they intended me, for by this time I could speak Spanish well enough to make myself understood."

Byron may have come to regret spurning the powerful uncle's offer, because on January 2, 1743, he and his comrades were transferred to Valparaiso, where the officers were placed in custody at St. Jago and he and Campbell were thrown into a horrific jail. Not only did they have to endure rats and lice, they were also harassed nearly daily by visitors who paid good money to come and look at them, so terrible were the reputations of Englishmen. After a time, some of these same people became so sympathetic to their plight that they actually began to bring them food and small amounts of cash, with which they were eventually able to buy their way into more comfortable surroundings in Santiago.

It seems that Byron's charms once more came to their aid, as Campbell later noted: "The Spaniards are very proud, and dress extremely gay; particularly the women, who spend a great deal of money upon their persons and houses. They are a good sort of people, and very courteous to strangers. Their women are also fond of gentlemen from other countries, and of other nations."

After two years living among the Spanish, the four men finally had the chance to head home, but Campbell refused to travel with the others because he had fallen out with Cheap over money. Thus, while Cheap, Hamilton, and Byron set sail on March 1, 1745 on the *Lys*, a French ship,

Campbell chose "to embark in a Spanish man-of-war then lying at Buenos Aires."

Cheap and his party made it as far as Brest, in France, before once again being abandoned. From there, it took them six months to find passage back to England but they finally made it home on April 9, 1745.

This left only the poor souls at Freshwater Bay still unaccounted for, but they too would live to tell their tales. They lived in Patagonia for a month, surviving by killing and eating the seals along the coast. Rested and strengthened by a steady diet of protein, they began an arduous 300 mile journey to Buenos Aires, fearful the entire trip of the Tehuelche Indians who lived in the area. At one point, they managed to walk 60 miles in two days, only to have to turn around and return to the bay because they could find no water inland.

The marooned survivors remained there until May 1742, by which time the seals had become fearful of humans and were no longer so easy to kill. At this point, they decided that they were likely going to live out the rest of their lives there, so they managed to trap some wild pigs that they bred and domesticated. This plan seem to be working until the predatory cats on the island got scent of penned up meat and began stalking the men's village.

While these four legged enemies made the men nervous, they were actually in more danger from the two-legged variety. Weeks later, a hunting party returned to camp to find that the men left behind had been murdered and the camp itself ransacked. This was enough to compel the four men who survived to quickly pack up what little they had left and start out again for Buenos Aires, this time with two pigs and 16 dogs they had managed to tame and raise.

Once again, they were forced to return to the bay, and again they tried to make lives for themselves there, but this time, the men who had previously attacked their camp returned and captured the four Englishmen to hold as slaves. Considered something of a novelty, they were owned by a number of men before finally becoming part of the household of the chief of the tribe. The chief managed to communicate with them enough to learn that they were English and sworn enemies of Spain. Since he was also at war with the Spaniards, he felt a kinship with them and provided better care for them. By the time 1743 came to a close, they had convinced him to help them return to England. He agreed, though he insisted that he would keep one of them, a mulatto named John Duck, in his household. At around this time, another Englishman, a trader, heard about the three who wanted to go home and paid the chief $90 each to release them.

This apparent salvation was short lived. When the men arrived in Buenos Aires, they were arrested again, this time by the Spanish governor, who demanded that they become Catholic. A few months later, in early 1745, a Spanish warship made it into port and took the men prisoners, chaining them up with a diet of bread and water for more than three months before releasing them.

In a strange twist of fate, Campbell himself arrived in Buenos Aires at about this time, having finally completed his harrowing, five month long trek across the Andes. He, too, was jailed by the Spanish, but he decided to convert to Catholicism, if only to enjoy better food and wine. He then used his influence to arrange passage home for himself, Morris, Cooper and Andrews.

The four men left for Spain in late October 1745, on board the *Asia*, where the three had previously been held prisoner. Incredibly, the men got a taste of déjà vu when 11 Indian crewmen mutinied and killed or injured 40 Spanish crewmen, but with a crew of more than 500, the captain was able to take back control, killing the chief mutineer and inspiring the others to jump overboard and, presumably, drown.

When the *Asia* finally arrived in Corcubion in January 1746, the Spanish authorities once more threw Morris, Andrews and Cooper in jail, and they hauled Campbell inland to Madrid. This led to rumors flying that Campbell had actually defected to the Spanish Navy, but he ultimately returned to England in May 1746, less than two months before his three other comrades finally made it home. Nonetheless, Campbell was still drummed out of the thoroughly Protestant British Navy because of his newfound religion. He blamed Cheap for much of his hard luck and later wrote, "Most of the hardships I suffered in following the fortunes of Captain Cheap were the consequence of my voluntary attachment to that gentleman. In reward for this the Captain has approved himself the greatest Enemy I have in the world. His ungenerous Usage of me forced me to quit his Company, and embark for Europe in a Spanish ship rather than a French one."

Chapter 6: Court Martials and the Aftermath

Naturally, when he got back, Captain Cheap wasted no time in going to the Admiralty and demanding that Bulkley be court martialed. The Admiralty readily agreed and ordered all those involved with the case to report to the HMS *Prince George*, anchored at Spithead, for the proceedings.

Ever the sneak, Bulkley invited the Deputy Marshal of the Admiralty to dinner but neglected to give him his real name. Bulkley later recalled what he said to him at dinner: "Desiring to know his opinion in regard to the Officers of the Wager, as their Captain was come home; for that I had a near relation which was an Officer that came in the long-boat from Brazil, and it would give me concern if he would suffer: His answer was that he believ'd that we should be hang'd [sic]. To which I replied, for God's Sake for what, for not being drown'd? And is a Murderer at last come home to their Accuser? I have carefully perused the Journal, and can't conceive that they have been guilty of Piracy, Mutiny, nor any Thing else to deserve it. It looks to me as if their Adversaries have taken up arms against the Power of the Almighty, for delivering them." According to Bulkley, the Deputy Marshal replied, "Sir, they have been guilty of such things to Captain Cheap whilst a Prisoner, that I believe the Gunner and Carpenter will be hang'd if no Body else." Thinking he had found an ally, Bulkley then admitted his true identity, only to learn that he had overplayed his hand, for the Deputy Marshal arrested him on the spot and transported him to the *Prince George*.

Vice Admiral James Stuart opened the proceedings on Tuesday, April 15, 1746. A number of witnesses came forward and told the story of what happened during the events leading up to Patagonia, but Cheap decided, under the advice of counsel, not to go after Bulkley and the others, for fear that this would raise the issue of Cozens' murder. The men in turn insisted that since they could no longer be paid after the *Wager* was wrecked, they were no longer obligated to obey orders. Captain S.W.C. Pack later wrote his own record of the trial and observed, "Their Lordships knew that a conviction of mutiny would be unpopular with the country. Things were bad with the Navy in April 1746. Their Lordships were out of favour. ... The defence that the Mutineers had was that as their wages automatically stopped when the ship was lost, they were no longer under naval law. Existence of such a misconception could lead, in time of enemy action or other hazard, to anticipation that the ship was already lost."

A decision supporting this theory could result in serious repercussions during a time of war, when men captured might claim that they no longer owed their country allegiance. In fact, Anson, who became a Lord Commissioner the following year, pushed through an Act that declared 'for extending the discipline of the Navy to crews of his majesty's ships, wrecked lost or taken, and continuing to receive wages upon certain conditions...''

In the end, it wasn't the law that saved the mutineers but simply the fact that the British public, which had been so taken with the survival stories, clearly did not favor strict punishment. Pack concluded, "Their Lordships knew that a conviction of mutiny would be unpopular with the country. Things were bad with the Navy in April 1746. Their Lordships were out of favour. One of the reasons for this was their harsh treatment of Admiral Vernon, a popular figure with the public... The defence that the Mutineers had was that as their wages automatically stopped when the ship was lost, they were no longer under naval law. Existence of such a misconception could lead, in time of enemy action or other hazard, to anticipation that the ship was already lost. Anson realised the danger and corrected this misconception. As Lord Commissioner he removed any further doubt in 1747. An Act was passed 'for extending the discipline of the Navy to crews of his majesty's ships, wrecked lost or taken, and continuing to receive wages upon certain conditions... The survivors of the Wager were extremely lucky not to be convicted of mutiny and owe their acquittal not only to the unpopularity of the Board, but to the strength of public opinion, to the fact that their miraculous escapes had captured the public fancy."

Thus, one by one the mutineers were acquitted until only Baynes remained accused, not of mutiny but of failure to carry out his duty and save the ship from floundering in the first place. However, the Admiralty was inclined to sweep even that matter under the rug. Their decision ultimately declared that "the Court, having maturely considered the case of Lieutenant Baynes, are unanimously of opinion that he was to blame in not acquainting the Captain when the Carpenter told him he thought he saw the land, in never heaving the lead, nor letting go the anchor…"

Moreover, the judges were men who in their time had faced all sorts of dangers, and they noted there were mitigating circumstances, including "the weakly condition of the ship, the cable being foul, and but thirteen sickly hands to clear it, as well as the little reason he appeared to have to believe it could have been the land which the Carpenter fancied he saw, either from its appearance, or from the distance his own & the general reckonings of the ship made them from the land…" As a result, "the Court do adjudge him the said Robert Baynes to be acquitted for the loss of the said ship Wager, but to be reprimanded by the President for such omission, & he is hereby acquitted accordingly, & ordered to be reprimanded."

For his part, Cheap was considered a hero, his treatment of Cozens considered secondary to his devotion to duty and his loyalty to the crown. The Admiralty promoted him to Post Captain, a rank that put him on the fast track for Admiral. He captured a large enemy ship in 1748, and the booty awarded to him from that ship made him a wealthy man. He had little time to enjoy his riches, however, as he died in 1752.

The other men were equally unlucky. Baynes' career at sea ended with the *Wager*, and he died in 1758. Bulkley was offered another ship but turned it down, insisting it was "too small to keep to the sea." He subsequently faded from history. Campbell, it seems, left the British Navy and threw his lot in with the Spaniards, though he later denied such claims.

Over 250 years later, it is Byron who is perhaps the most famous crewmember. He was promoted to Master and Commander, and given the command of the *Syren*. He lived a long life, during which he sailed around the world before his death in 1786. He was also married and had a number of children whom he lived to see grow up. They in turn had children of their own, one of whom grew up to be one of Britain's most famous Romantic poets: Lord Byron. The dashing young poet certainly had a spirit as adventurous as his legendary grandfather, and he would suffer trials and tribulations in war as well, dying in Greece while fighting against the Turks in the Greek War of Independence.

Lord Byron

For decades following the loss of the *Wager*, Spain controlled the area in which the ship was wrecked and was not terribly inclined to allow English explorers in to look for her. Archaeologist Diego Carabias Amor wrote that, sometime around 1743, "the Governor of Chiloe...organiz[ed] an important salvage operation to recover the guns, anchors and nautical gear of the Wager, all of which were very scarce in the region.... The objects recovered included ten iron six-pounder and four bronze three-pounder guns, an anchor, over a hundred cannon balls, over a thousand musket shot, three copper cauldrons, and various pieces of lead, iron and steel."

Having gotten all that they could use from the ship, the Spanish quickly lost interest in the wreck, and it was allowed to remain largely unmolested in the decades that followed. Men exploring the area would occasionally make reference to finding parts of the ship, but there was no concerted effort made to explore or salvage it.

In 2006, over 250 years after the ship was wrecked, the Scientific Exploration Society asked Major Chris Holt to lead a team in search of the *Wager*. The team flew out of England on November 5 and made their way to Patagonia, accomplishing in hours what it had taken Anson and his men months to do. Once there, he tried a number of sites before demanding that the team get back to basics. He confided to his journal, "We re-read the accounts (rather than the books about the accounts) and came up with the following pieces of information that we felt were important: . The ship was only 'feet from making clear water' and missing the island before she struck. 2. When the men first launched the lengthened long-boat Speedwell, they immediately turned away from the wind and across the 'inlet' to Speedwell Bay (something in the accounts we had somehow previously all missed)."

He gleaned one more piece of critical information: "3. From Mount Misery looking towards land (i.e. east), it was not possible to see if they were on an island because of greater hills in the way. All of these points lead us to believe we need to be not on the north-eastern but on the north-western shore."

Armed with this information, the team chose a new site in which to look, at the foot of what the sailors had called Mount Misery but had later been named Mount Anson. This proved to be the right place, as Holt later wrote in his report, "Andy [Torbet] is not someone who is drawn into false optimism; he is a 'professional Scotsman' and proud of it. When I met him back at the boats, he was excited about the correlation between what he had seen from the top of the mountain and the descriptions in the accounts. He finished off his debrief to me by saying: 'I think I've just been to the summit of Mount Misery, which means that the Wager is somewhere here.'"

Excited by this prediction, the entire team moved about their tasks quickly until one member cried out in pain after he had stubbed his toe on something. He called out to the others, "Just a minute fellas, I'm going to move this damned thing, otherwise I'll only do it again."

Holt described what happened next: "On his hands and knees, he cleared away the sand around the offending item and tried to move it away from his now throbbing toes. It was an unusual moment, one of those where everyone goes quiet at the same time and you cannot really remember who spoke first, but, as he continued to fan with his hand, slowly but surely the outline of a large worked piece of timber became visible...More hands joined his, and within three or four minutes we had uncovered about one and a half metres of hull planking. An unusual feeling came over me, much like when you have known the answer to a question all along, but for some reason have forgotten to tell anyone. We were literally ten metres away from my tent, in the very spot where for a week we had been washing our pots, pans, clothes and bodies, and it was entirely likely that we had just stumbled over the wreck of HMS Wager...The storm that had come close to washing away our morale had also scoured away large amounts of sand on the bottom of the stream, exposing the smallest edge of timbers that must have remained buried for decades."

There was too little time and not enough provisions to do more than excavate what they could and take some pictures. The site was visited again the following year, and more of the wreckage was found, but for the most part, the *Wager* still keeps her own counsel and lies, like the bodies of so many of her crew, on the shore and in the shallow waters off the Chilean coast.

HMS *Bounty*

Chapter 1: His Majesty's Armed Vessel the *Bounty*

A replica of the *Bounty*

"The Order from the Right Honorable Lords Commissioners of the Admiralty, dated the 20th. August last and directed to the President, representing that by an Order from the late Board of Admiralty dated the 16th. Of August, 1787, Lieutenant (now Captain) William Bligh was appointed to Command His Majesty's armed Vessel the "Bounty" and, by Instructions from the same Board dated the 20th. November in the same year, was directed to proceed in that Vessel to the Society Islands in order to procure and transport from thence to some of the British

Possessions in the West Indies Bread Fruit Trees and other useful Plants, the produce of the said Islands, and further representing that the said Lieutenant Bligh sailed from Spithead on the 23rd. of December following in prosecution of his destined Voyage…" – Excerpt from the "Court-Martial On Board His Majesty's Ship Duke in Portsmouth, Wednesday, 12th September, 1792"

Like so many of history's tragedies, the mutiny on the *Bounty* ultimately came about because of the great evil that was slavery. In the 1780s, slavery was a common practice in the British West Indies, and feeding the increasing number of slaves working on far-flung plantations was a constant source of concern. Thus, on May 5, 1787, Lord Sydney, the Home Secretary, issued the following instructions: "Lords Commissioners of the Admiralty, My Lords, The Merchants and Planters interested in His Majesty's West India Possessions have represented that the Introduction of the Bread Fruit Tree into those Islands to constitute an article of Food would be of very essential benefit to the inhabitants, and have humbly solicited that measures might be taken for procuring some Trees of that description from the place of their present growth to be transplanted in the said Islands ... some able and discreet officer ... half the plants to St Vincent ... other half to Jamaica"

Breadfruit is a common and very nutritious plant easily grown in the tropics, so the thinking was that if more plants could be transferred to the West Indian plantations, they could supply a steady diet for the workers. With that in mind, the Royal Navy took the *Bethia*, a ship they had recently purchased in 1787 for £1950, and renamed her the HMS *Bounty*. Captain William Bligh had a long and solid career in Britain's Royal Navy, and on August 16 of that year, he was appointed to the task of sailing the *Bounty* to Tahiti to acquire breadfruit trees and deliver to the West Indies. He later wrote:

> "The Burthen of the Ship was nearly 215 Tons; Her extreme length on deck 90Ft. 10In. and breadth from outside to outside of the bends 24Ft. 3 in. A Flush deck and a pretty Figure Head of a Woman in Riding habit; She mounted 4 four pounders and 10 Swivels and her Complement was,
>
> 1 Lieutenant and Commander
>
> 2 Masters Mates
>
> 1 Gunners Mate
>
> 1 Master
>
> 2 Midshipmen
>
> 1 Carpenters Mate
>
> 1 Boatswain

1 Clerk

1 Sail maker

1 Gunner

2 Quarter Masters

1 Armorer

1 Carpenter

1 Quarter Master Mate

1 Carpenters Crew

1 Surgeon

1 Boatswains Mate

1 Corporal

24 Able Seamen

Total. 45 One of which is a Widow's man. There was likewise a Botanist David Nelson and his Assistant."

Bligh

An illustration depicting the crew of the *Bounty* handling breadfruit trees

After inspecting his new command, Bligh requested that the ship's masts and yard arms be cut down, hoping to improve her sailing ability, but the *Bounty* seemed to be cursed with bad luck from the very moment Bligh took command. On October 15, 1787, he and his new crew sailed from Deptford, England, where the ship had been refitted, to Spithead, arriving later than they were supposed to because of bad weather along the way. Due to this delay and others, the *Bounty* was much later in leaving England than it ought to have been, finally getting under way on December 23.

As fate would have it, bad luck followed the *Bounty* out to sea. James Morrison, the boatswain's mate, recalled, "On the 9th of September 1787 I entered on board His Majesty's Armed Vessel *Bounty*, Lieut. Wm. Bligh Commander, then lying at Deptford. On the 18 9th October following she dropped down to long reach and in a few days after sailed for Spithead where she anchored on the 4th of November and after several attempts in one of which the Fore topsail Yard was carried away, (which together with a cable that was rubbed at St. Helens were returned at Portsmouth Yard and new ones got in their stead) she sailed on the 23rd of December with a fresh Gale Easterly, which Increased to a heavy Gale by the 27th in which the Ships Oars a spare Topsail yard and Top Galt Yard were washed from the Quarters one of the

Eye Bolts being drawn from the side. She also shipped a sea, which broke the Boats Chock and tore all the planks from the large Cutters Stem, and washed some empty Casks overboard which were on the Deck; another Sea stove in a part of the stem between the deadlights, but did very little other Damage except breaking an Azimuth Compass and wetting a few bags of bread in the Cabin; the breach in the stem was soon secured, and the Ship hove to, as it became dangerous to Scud."

Though the weather continued to be a problem, the *Bounty* arrived safely at the Canary Islands on January 5, 1788 and left there on January 10 with supplies for the next leg of her journey. A few weeks later, on March 2, Bligh promoted Master's Mate Fletcher Christian, whom he had particularly requested join him on the voyage, to the rank of acting lieutenant.

Two weeks later, the *Bounty* began to try to make passage around the treacherous Cape Horn. A difficult feat in the best of times, it proved to be impossible in the conditions the *Bounty* encountered, and on April 22, Blight was forced to give up and sail instead toward Africa. Bligh later wrote,

> "At last seeing eight of my Men not able to Duty from severe Rheumatisms, two with dislocated shoulders and one with a broken rib, and the rest being but few much harassed and fatigued from the severity of the weather, the ropes being worked and Sails furled with much difficulty from the heavy snow storms, I was obliged to give way, but it was from the following reasons.
>
> That it appeared evidently I had but little chance to accomplish my passage during the time I could possibly stay longer in this Sea.
>
> That to put into Port at such a season and attempt it again, provided I had success was gaining but little time and the chance much against me.
>
> That I had not a moment to spare to make my passage to the Cape of Good Hope and refit so as to secure my getting to Otaheitein time.
>
> That the Ship from being constantly in very high Seas began to be leaky and required carefully to be attended with the pumps, and increased our labor.
>
> That my People now being but ten on whom the hard Duty of furling and reefing principally fell upon, felt much the severity of the weather and were much harassed and fatigued and might soon fall sick, and in this case failing after all I thereby endangered the grand pursuit of the Voyage, and I became reprehensible having discretionary orders…to go by way of Cape Horn.
>
> That upon the whole, the one amounting the matter to a certainty and the other to a doubt I made my mind up on the first being the only one eligible however it

may prove successful."

Bligh's decision was positively received. According to James Morrison, "April, 1788. On the 18th of April Mr. Bligh ordered all hands aft and after returning them his thanks for their unremitted attention to their duty, informed them of his intention to bear away for the Cape of Good Hope; as it appeared to him an Impossibility to get round Cape Horn. This was received with Universal Joy and returned according to Custom with three Cheers…A hog was now killed and served out in lieu of the day's allowance, which though scarce anything else but skin and bone was greedily devoured; every one by this time being fairly Come to their Appetites…After we bore away we got the Hatches opened which we could not very often do before, being forced to keep them almost constantly battened down. We also got the stoves to work airing and drying the Ship between decks, and the sick recovered fast, as we got into a more temperate Climate."

The *Bounty* reached Simon's Bay along the Cape of Good Hope in Africa on May 24, 1788 and began resupplying. A few days later, with the crew rested and the ship fully supplied, Bligh set sail again, safely arriving at Adventure Bay in Tasmania on August 21 and, after taking on more supplies, set sail again on September 4. Finally, the ship arrived at her destination, Matavai Bay in Tahiti, on October 25, 1788.

Chapter 2: He Frequently Threatened Them

A painting depicting the Bounty

"They declare that Captain Bligh used to call his officers 'scoundrels, damned rascals, hounds, hell-hounds, beasts, and infamous wretches'; that he frequently threatened them, that when the ship arrived at Endeavor Straits, 'he would kill one half of the people, make the officers jump overboard, and would make them eat grass like cows'; and that Christian, and Stewart, another midshipman, were as much afraid of Endeavour Straits, as any child is of a rod. Captain Bligh was accustomed to abuse Christian much more frequently and roughly than the rest of the officers, or as one of the persons expressed it, 'whatever fault was found, Mr. Christian was sure to bear the brunt of the Captain's anger.' In speaking to him in this violent manner, Captain Bligh frequently 'shook his fist in Christian's face.'" - Edward Christian, brother of Fletcher Christian

On November 2, 1788, Bligh sent out the first team of nine men to harvest the breadfruit trees, but it was also around this same time that problems began to erupt among the crew. Bligh had always been a stern commander, but most 18th century captains were, but while there had been several incidents during the voyage that compelled him to order a man lashed for various misdeeds, once the crew settled in Tahiti, the misdeeds, and accompanying punishments, became more frequent. For instance, on November 4, the captain complained, "Several petty Thefts having been committed by the Natives owing to the negligence and inattention of the Petty Officers and Men, which has always more or less a tendency to alarm the Chiefs. I was under the necessity this afternoon to punish Alex Smith with 12 lashes for suffering the Gudgeon of the large Cutter to be drawn out without knowing it. Several Chiefs were on board at the time, and with their wives interceded for the Man, but seeing it had no effect they retired; and the women in general showed every degree of Sympathy which marked them to be the most humane and affectionate creatures in the World."

It's possible that this scene alerted the men to the idea that their captain was not as all-powerful or worthy of their allegiance as they were taught he was in the English speaking world. Then, a month later, on December 5, Bligh wrote, "In the afternoon I directed the Carpenter to cut a large stone that was brought off by one of the Natives, (Odiddee) requesting me to get it made fit for them to grind their Hatchets on, but to my astonishment he refused to comply in direct terms saying "I will not cut the stone for it will spoil my Chisel, and though there is law to take away my clothes there is none to take away my Tools". This Man having before shown his mutinous and insolent behavior: I was under the necessity to confine him to his Cabin. Although I can but ill spare the loss of a single Man, but I do not intend to lose the use of him but remit him to his duty tomorrow. ... Punished Mathew Thompson with 12 lashes for insolence and disobedience of orders."

As 1788 was coming to a close, it seems there was a downward spiral in Bligh's behavior, especially as he seemed to be losing control over his crew. To make matters worse, Bligh seemed to have no one to turn to that he could trust; often a captain might find friendship with the ship's surgeon since that man does not often have to take orders, but Blight despised the surgeon on the *Bounty*, John Huggan. On December 10, Bligh wrote of the surgeon, "This unfortunate man died owing to drunkenness and indolence. Exercise was a thing he could not bear an Idea of, or could I ever bring him to take a half dozen of turns on deck at a time in the course of the whole Voyage. Sleeping was the way he spent his time, and he accustomed himself to breathe so little fresh air and was so filthy in his person that he became latterly a nuisance."

Though Thomas Ledward, whom Bligh appointed to replace Huggan, would prove to be a more faithful crewman, there was little he could do to control Bligh's temper and outbursts. Instead, things went from bad to worse as more and more men were found wanting and punished severely. A more mature man might have been able to wonder if the fault lay with him, but at the age of 34, Bligh had apparently not yet developed a talent for self-evaluation and correction. Instead, he became more and more determined to see his will done.

On January 5, 1789, three men deserted the ship, taking a cutter ashore and disappearing into the Tahitian jungle. Discussing their desertion, Bligh wrote:

> "At the relief of the watch at four o'clock this morning the small cutter was missing. I was immediately informed of it and mustered the ship's company, when it appeared that three men were absent: Charles Churchill, the ship's corporal and two of the seamen, William Musprat and John Millward, the latter of whom had been sentinel from twelve to two in the morning. They had taken with them eight stand of arms and ammunition; but what their plan was, or which way they had gone, no one on board seemed to have the least knowledge. I went on shore to the chiefs and soon received information that the boat was at Matavai; and that the deserters had departed in a sailing canoe for the island Tethuroa. On this intelligence I sent the master to Matavai to search for the small cutter, and one of the chiefs went with him; but before they had got halfway they met the boat with five of the natives who were bringing her back to the ship. This service rendered me by the people of Matavai pleased me much and I rewarded the men accordingly.
>
> I told Tinah and the other chiefs that I expected they would get the deserters brought back; for that I was determined not to leave Otaheite without them. They assured me that they would do everything in their power to have them taken and it was agreed that Oreepyah and Moannah should depart the next morning for Tethuroa. Oreepyah enquired if they had pocket pistols 'for,' said he, 'though we may surprise and seize them before they can make use of their muskets, yet if they have pistols they may do mischief, even while they are held.' I quietened these apprehensions by assuring them that the deserters had no pistols with them."

The men were indeed found on January 23, 1789, and they were duly punished, but by this time, Bligh had a new set of problems because the ship's sails were damaged. He confided to his logbook, "This Morning the sail Room being cleared to take the sails on shore to Air, The New Fore Topsail and Foresail, Main Top Staysail and Main Staysail were found very much mildewed and rotten in many places. If I had any Officers to supersede the Master and Boatswain, or was capable of doing without them considering them as common seamen, they should no longer occupy their respective Stations. Scarce any neglect of duty can equal the criminality of this, for it appears that although the Sails have been taken out twice since I have been in the Island, which I thought fully sufficient and I had trusted to their reports, yet these New Sails never were brought out, or is it certain whether they have been out since we left England, yet notwithstanding as often as the Sails were taken to air by my Orders they were reported to me to be in good Order. To remedy the defects I attended and saw the Sails put into the Sea and hung up on shore to dry to be ready for repairing."

He then added ruefully, "Cleaned ship and got up all chests to clear the Cockroaches Smoked with Tobacco."

Over the next several months, the floggings were increasingly reported in Bligh's logbook. It is impossible in hindsight to know with any certainty exactly what was going on, but something was obviously going very wrong on the *Bounty*. By the time the men had collected all the breadfruit trees the ship could hold and preparations were made to sail on April 4, 1789, the stage was set for disaster. It was just a question of when it would begin to play out.

Chapter 3: Mr. Christian Had Taken the Ship

A picture of Clark Gable as Fletcher Christian in *Mutiny on the Bounty* (1935)

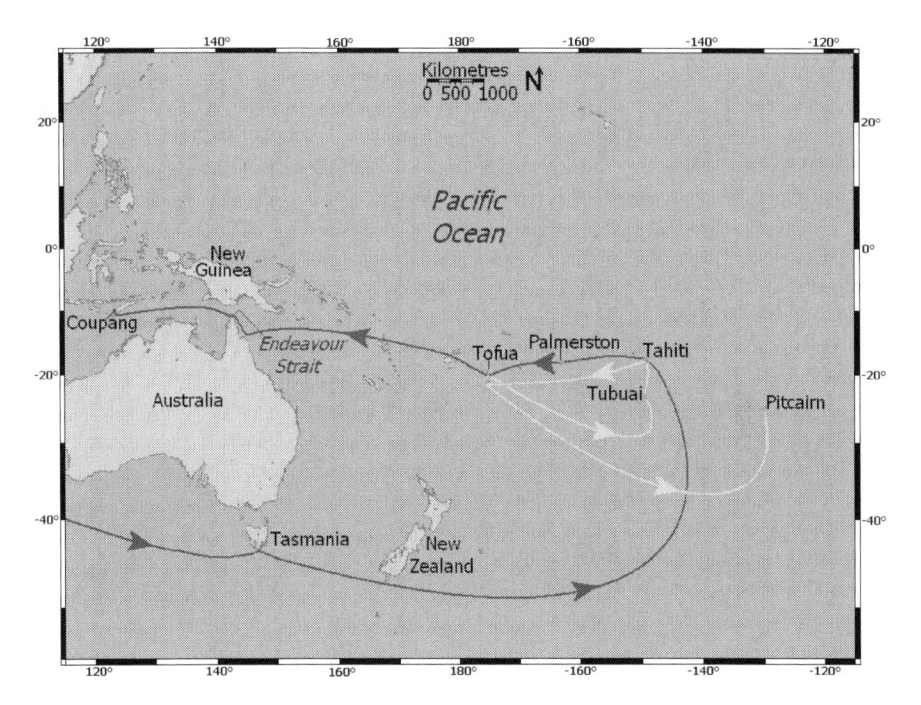

The route of the *Bounty*, with the mutineers' course in yellow and the adrift crew in green

"On the Twenty Eight of April at day break the Captain and me were surprised by Mr. Christian, Stewart Young Haywood and the Master at Arms, with twenty one people. Christian and the Master at Arms went into Mr. Bligh's Cabin and tied his hands behind him. Two men came into my Cabin, with muskets and Bayonets, told me if I spoke, that I was a dead man and that Mr. Christian had taken the Ship and that they was to put us onshore upon one of the Friendly Isles. I expostulated with them but all to no purpose, they hoisted the long boat out, and all them that would not join with them in the Mutiny, they obliged to go into the boat. I was the last that received that order and I was obliged to beg hard of Christian to let Robert come with me — he at last consented that he could come with me. — When I came on deck I found they had forced…seven of the men into the boat with the Captain which with Robert and myself made nineteen." - John Fryer, Master of the Bounty

Things on the *Bounty* came to a head on April 28, 1789. Peter Heywood, one of those later captured and tried for mutiny, wrote, "On the preceding Evening at eight o Clock, PM— I went upon Deck, and kept the first Watch, with Mr. John Fryer, the Master, who ordered me to keep the Cook out upon the Forecastle, and remained there till past twelve o Clock, when I was relieved by Mr. Edward Young a Midshipman; upon which I went down below into my Birth, which was on the larboard side of the main Hatchway, and slept in my Hammock, till about an Hour after Day-light, (perhaps it might be sooner, I cannot positively tell); when I awoke, and laying my Cheek upon the side of my Hammock, chanced to look into the main Hatchway, where I saw Mathew Thompson, Seaman, sitting upon an Arm Chest, which was there secured; with a drawn Cutlass in his Hand; — and as I knew him to be a man who had kept the middle Watch with Mr. William Peckover the Gunner, I was struck with surprise, at a sight so unusual; unable to conjecture the reason of his being there at so early an Hour — I immediately got out of Bed, went to the side of the Birth, and asked him what he was doing there? Upon which he replied — "that Mr. Fletcher Christian, who had the Watch upon Deck, had taken the ship from the Captain whom he had confined upon Deck; and was going to carry him Home as a Prisoner, and that they should have more Provisions, and better Usage than before" — Mr. Elphinstone, one of the Master's Mates, who was then lying awake in his Hammock, which hung at the outside of the opposite Birth and likewise heard what this Man said to me."

A portrait believed to depict Heywood

Months later, Bligh told his side of the story in a letter to his wife: "On the 28th April at day light in the morning Christian having the morning watch, He with several others came into my Cabin while I was a Sleep, and seizing me, holding naked Bayonets at my Breast, tied my Hands behind my back, and threatened instant destruction if I uttered a word. I however called loudly for assistance, but the conspiracy was so well laid that the Officers Cabin Doors were guarded by Sentinels, so that Nelson, Peckover, Samuels or the Master could not come to me. I was now dragged on Deck in my Shirt and closely guarded—I demanded of Christian the cause of such a violent act, and severely degraded him for his Villainy but he could only answer—"not a word Sir or you are Dead." I dared him to the act and endeavored to rally someone to a sense of their duty but to no effect. Besides this Villain see young Heywood, one of the ringleaders, and besides him see Stewart joined with him. Christian I had assured of promotion when he came home, and with the other two I was every day rendering them some service—It is incredible! These very young Men I placed every confidence in, yet these great Villains joined with the most able Men in the Ship got possession of the Arms and took the *Bounty* from me, with huzzahs for Otaheite. I have now reason to curse the day I ever knew a Christian or a Heywood or indeed a Manksman."

James Morrison was one of the last men to learn what had happened:

> "The night being Calm we made no way, and in the Morning of the 28th the Boatswain Came to my hammock and waked me telling me to my great surprise that the ship was taken by Mr. Christian. I hurried on deck and found it true —seeing Mr. Bligh in his shirt with his hands tied behind him and Mr. Christian standing by him with a drawn Bayonet in his hand and his Eyes flaming with revenge. Several of the men were under arms, and the Small Cutter hoisted out, and the large one getting ready.
>
> I applied to the Boatswain [Cole] to know how I should proceed, but he was as much at a loss as I, and in a Confused Manner told me to lend a hand in Clearing the Boat and Getting her out, which I did, when she was out the Small one was got in— Mr. Christian called to Mr. Hayward and Mr. Hallet to get into the Boat and ordered Churchill to See the Master [Fryer] and Clerk [Samuel] into Her. The Lieutenant then began to reason but Mr. Christian replied 'Mamoo, Sir, not a word, or deaths your portion'. Mr. Hayward and Mr. Hallet begged with tears in their eyes to be suffered to remain in the ship but Mr. Christian ordered them to be silent. The Boatswain and Carpenter [Purcell] Came aft (the Master and Gunner [Peckover] being Confined below) and begged for the Launch, which with much hesitation was Granted, and she was ordered out."

In that moment, many of the men on the ship faced several life or death decisions. Captain Bligh had to decide if he should throw himself entirely to keeping his ship or agree to be marooned, and while the first choice would've brought certain death, the other was nearly as dangerous. Meanwhile, others had to decide whether to resist the mutineers or go along. Morrison remembered, "While I was Clearing her the Master Came up and spoke to Mr. Bligh and afterwards Came to Me, asking me if I had any hand in the Mutiny—I told him I had not, and he then desired me to try what I Could do to raise a party and rescue the Ship, which I promised to do. In consequence of which John Millward who was by me at the time Swore he would stand by me, and went to Musprat, Burket and the Boatswain on that score, but Churchill seeing the Master speaking to me (though he was Instantly hurried away by Quintrell ordering him down to his Cabin) Came and demanded what he had said. I told him that He was asking about the Launch but Alex Smith who stood on the other side of the Boat told Churchill to look sharp after me saying 'tis a damned lye, Chas, for I saw him and Millward shake hands, when the Master spoke to them, and Called to the others to stand to their Arms, which put them on their Guard'."

For many, the confusion of the moment proved too much, especially since the crew members who were surprised by the mutiny had minutes to make the type of decision that would normally take days to consider. Peter Heywood explained, "Mr. Christian…was giving Orders to Mr. Cole the Boatswain, (who was upon Deck) to hoist the large Cutter out, the small one having been got out some time before. — upon this I came a little farther forward, and went over to the other side, and saw Mr. Christian beckon to Mr. Thos. Hayward (who with Mr. Hallet was standing on the Quarter Deck, between the two four Pounders,) he said to him — 'get yourself ready to go in the Boat Sir' — and Mr. Hayward made Answer —'why? Mr. Christian what Harm did I ever do you?, that you should be so hard upon me, I hope you won't insist upon it' — but he again repeated the same Order to him, and to Mr. John Hallet, who seemed to be in Tears, and answered, — 'I hope not Sir' — hearing this, and being afraid that if I was in his Sight, he might give me the same Orders, which I feared very much, because I had just before asked one of the Men whom I saw with a Musket in his Hand, why they were getting the Boats out? — he answered — 'that the Capitan. with some Individuals, were to be sent on shore at Tofoa, in the Launch, and that he believed that all the rest who were not of Mr. Christians Party, might either accompany them in the Launch, or remain on board and be carried to 'Tahiti and left on Shore there among the Natives, as they were going there with the ship to procure Provisions, Refreshments, and Stock, to take to some unknown Island, to make a settlement.'"

Picture of the *Bounty*'s rudder on display in Fiji

Chapter 4: A Most Distressed Situation

"The Misery of this day has exceeded the preceding. The night was dreadful. The Sea flew over us with great force and kept us bailing with horror and anxiety. At Dawn of day I found everyone in a most distressed situation, and I now began to fear that another such night would produce the End of several who were no longer able to bear it. Every one complained of Severe Bone Aches which was cured in some measure by about two Spoonfuls of Rum, and having wrung our clothes and taken our breakfast of Bread and water we became a little refreshed. Towards noon it came fair but very little abatement of the Gale and the Sea equally high. With great difficulty I got an observation." - Captain Bligh, May 23, 1789

As the mutiny quickly unfolded, the group of men who had functioned as a single unit for nearly two years were split in two. The mutineers and those that joined them would remain on the ship and try to find a place where they could live without being discovered for who they were, while those who stood with Captain Bligh would be set afloat on a cutter with enough provisions to reach the nearest island. Most of the men already had their minds made up, but even at this point, a few were waffling. Peter Heywood described his own state of mind at the time: "Hearing a Scheme of such pre-concerted Determination, of which I had not the least Conception, — I was so perplexed and astonished that I knew not what to do or think, but sat down on the gunnel of the ship, on the Starboard side, just under the fore Shrouds, and weighed the Difference of these two dreadful Alternatives in my Mind: — I considered that the Indians on shore at Tofoa…appeared to me to be a very savage sort of People when unawed by the sight of Fire Arms, and from whom naught but Death could be expected…and besides I considered that a small Boat, deeply laden, with a number of Men and Provisions for the Sustenance, would be a very precarious and forlorn Hope to trust Life to, in sailing across so vast an expanse of Ocean as lay between this Island and the nearest civilized Port; that in pursuing this Plan, Death appeared to me to be inevitable in its most horrid, and dreadful Form of starving. — On the other Hand, I knew the Natives of 'Tahiti to be a remarkably friendly and hospitable People to Strangers, by whose kind Assistance and Benevolence, I had some Hopes, if I could get there that my Life might be preserved, till a ship arrived from England. … This was the only Means which appeared to me to render a possibility of ever returning to my Native Country, or even of preserving my Life. — Thus, self-preservation, that first Law of Nature, was the only Motive that induced me to resolve upon the last Alternative."

Thus, Heywood remained on the *Bounty* with Christian, while Bligh, Ledward and several others were ordered into the cutter. Just before the open boat was left, several more men chose to join them rather than remain with the mutineers. According to Bligh, "The Officers and Men being now drove into the Boat One by One. I was told by Christian, "Sir, your officers are now in the Boat and you must go with them. I was then taken hold of under a Guard, and forced over the Gangway into the Boat, which waited only for me, and untying my Hands I was veered astern by a Rope. A few Pounds of Pork were now thrown to us being nineteen in number and each began to solicit some of their little Valuables that were left behind them. I desired only some Fire Arms and even at last solicited two but we received insolence and were told I should have none, Four Cutlasses were however thrown into the Boat and we were cast adrift and Rowed with all our strength for the land. The Size of the Boat was 23 feet from Stem to Stern and Rowed Six Oars, and was so deeply lumbered that they believed we could never reach the Shore and some of them made their Jokes of it, However by 7 o'clock in the Evening I got safe under Tofoa, but could find no landing, and therefore kept the Boat under the land all night paddling with Two Oars to preserve our station."

Bligh's document naming the mutineers, with Fletcher Christian's name at the top

The following day, Bligh's group was already worrying about supplies. He noted, "Endeavoring to find landing to increase our Stock of Water, and to get some Cocoa Nuts and Provisions." Then, according to Bligh, "About ten o'clock we discovered a cove with a stony beach at the north-west part of the island, where I dropped the grapnel within 20 yards of the rocks. A great surf ran on the shore but, as I was unwilling to diminish our stock of provisions, I landed Mr. Samuel and some others, who climbed the cliffs and got into the country to search for supplies. The rest of us remained at the cove, not discovering any other way into the country than that by which Mr. Samuel had proceeded. ... Towards noon Mr. Samuel returned with a few quarts of water which he had found in holes; but he had met with no spring or any prospect of a sufficient supply in that particular, and had seen only the signs of inhabitants. As it was uncertain what might be our future necessities I only issued a morsel of bread and a glass of wine to each person for dinner."

Unfortunately, Bligh soon learned that the native people on Tofoa were not terribly happy to see him and his men arrive. In fact, they were quite hostile to the newcomers. Bligh later wrote that on May 2, 1789, "We all got into the boat except one man...I was no sooner in the boat than the attack began by about 200 men; the unfortunate poor man who had run up the beach was knocked down, and the stones flew like a shower of shot. ... We had no time to reflect for to my surprise they filled their canoes with stones, and twelve men came off after us to renew the attack, which they did so effectually as nearly to disable us all. ... They however could paddle round us, so that we were obliged to sustain the attack without being able to return it, except with such stones as lodged in the boat, and in this I found we were very inferior to them...I therefore adopted the expedient of throwing overboard some clothes which, as I expected, they stopped to pick up and, as it was by this time almost dark, they gave over the attack and returned towards the shore...The poor man killed by the natives was John Norton: this was his second voyage with me as a quartermaster, and his worthy character made me lament his loss very much." Thus, ironically, the first casualty of the mutiny was on an island miles away from Christian and the other mutineers.

For the next four weeks, the former officers of the *Bounty* and those who had thrown their lot in with them sailed in the cutter, carefully rationing their food and water in order to make it to land before both gave out. However, by May 26, nearly a month after the mutiny, their luck and their food were both running out. On that day, Bligh recorded, "In the Evening we saw several Boobies, and flying so near to us that we caught one of them by hand. This Bird is as large as a good duck...They are generally in the neighborhood of Land. I directed it to be killed for Supper and the blood was given to three of the most distressed for want of food. The body Entrails Beak and feet I divided into 18 shares and with an allowance of Bread which I made a merit of granting we made a good Supper."

Fortunately, just two days later, the men made landfall on Restoration Island in New Holland and Bligh was able to record, "In the morning at day light I bore away again for the Reefs and saw them by nine o'clock. ... I expected but little from the Oars because we had no Strength to pull them, and it was becoming every minute more and more probable that I should be obliged to take the Reef in case we could not pull off. ... Being now happily within the Reefs and Smooth water, I endeavored to keep hold of the Reef to fish, but the Tide set me to the NW. I therefore bore away in that direction, and having promised to land on the first convenient spot we could find, all our past hardships already seemed to be forgot."

Bligh had managed to navigate the ship an estimated 3600 nautical miles using little more than a quadrant and watch, but his travels were far from finished.

Chapter 5: Rescue the Ship

"The behavior of the Officers on this Occasion was dastardly beyond description none of them ever making the least attempt to rescue the ship which would have been effected had any attempt been made by one of them as some of those who were under arms did not know what they were about, and Robert Lamb who I found Sentry at the fore Hatchway when I first came on Deck went away in the Boat and Isaac Martin had laid his arms down and gone into the boat but had been Ordered out again." - James Morrison

Following Bligh's departure, Christian faced the daunting task of leading men already naturally inclined to insubordination, and on top of that, he still had to convince several of them that he was justified in his decision to mutiny. Furthermore, according to Morrison, Christian didn't initially plan to mutiny but instead simply wanted to desert the ship. Morrison later wrote, "Their passive obedience to Mr. Christians orders even surprised himself and he said immediately after the boat was gone that something more than fear had possessed them to suffer themselves to be sent away in such a manner without offering to make resistance. When the Boat Put off Mr. Stuart and Mr. Heywood who had been Confined in their birth came up and Mr. Christian related the Cause of this sad affair to the following effect—Finding himself much hurt by the treatment he had received from Mr. Bligh, he had determined to quit the ship the preceding evening, and informed the Boatswain, Carpenter, Mr. Stuart and Mr. Hayward of his resolution who supplied Him with some Nails, Beads and part of a roasted pig with some other articles which He put into a bag which He got from Mr. Hayward (the bag was produced and I knew it to be the same which I had made for Mr. Hayward some time before), the bag was put into the Clue of Robert Tinkler's hammock, where he found it at Night; but the Matter was then Smothered, and passed off—he also made fast some staves to a stout Plank which lay on the larboard Gangway, with which he intended to make his escape; but finding he could not effect it in the first and Middle Watches, as the people were all a stirring, he went to sleep about half past three in the Morning."

However, by the time the next day dawned, Christian learned that he was indeed not alone in his unhappiness. Morrison continued, "When Mr. Stuart called him to relieve the Watch he had not Slept long, and was much out of order, and Stuart begged him not to attempt swimming away, saying 'the People are ripe for anything', this made a forcible impression on his mind and finding that Mr. Hayward the Mate of his Watch (with whom he refused to discourse) soon went to sleep on the Arm Chest which stood between the Guns, and Mr. Hallet not making his appearance, He at once resolved to seize the ship and disclosing his Intention to Quintrell and Martin, they Calld up Churchill, and Thompson who put the business in practice and with Smith, Williams and McCoy He went to Coleman and demanded the Keys of the Arm Chest (which Coleman the Armorer always kept) saying he wanted a Musket to shoot a shark which happened to Come alongside; and finding Mr. Hallet asleep on the Arm Chest he roused him and sent him on Deck the keys were Instantly procured and His party armed, as were all the rest who stood in his way, without their knowing for what purpose. In the Meantime, Norman had Waked Mr. Hayward to look after the shark, at which He was busy when Mr. Christian Came up the fore Hatchway with his party, he left [Th]ompson to take Care of the Arm Chest, arming Burket [an]d Lamb at the Hatch way and Commanding Mr. Hayward and Mr. Hallet to be silent He proceeded to Secure Lieut. Bligh, whom He brought on Deck placing two sentries at the Masters Cabin door to keep him in, and keep the Gunner and Mr. Nelson in the Cockpit and proceeded as before described."

Later, Morrison claimed that he had tried to retake *Bounty* in the hope of returning it to the Royal Navy: "May, 1789. As I had reason to believe from the Countenance of Affairs that the Ship might yet be recovered if a party could be formed and as I knew that several on board were not at all pleased with their situation, I fixed on a Plan for that purpose and soon gained several to back my opinion, when We purposed to take the Opportunity of the Night the ship should anchor at Tahiti when we could easily get rid of those we did not like by putting them on shore, and that in all probability our design might be favored by an extra allowance of Grog. These matters being settled I had no doubt but that everyone would stand to the test; and to prevent the others from knowing our design affected a shyness toward each other, but I soon found to my unspeakable surprise that Mr. Christian was acquainted with our Intentions, some of his party overhearing some part of the Business—but as he was not positive how many were Concerned he took no further Notice then threatening Coleman that he should be left on shore at Toobouai till the Ship returned from Tahiti and Got the Arm Chest into the Cabin taking the Keys from Coleman who had always kept them; they were now given to Churchill who made his bed on the Chest and each of Mr. Christian's party were Armed with a Brace of Pistols, Mr. Christian himself never going without a Pistol in his pocket, the same which Lieut. Bligh formerly used, and a sharp look out was kept by his party one of which took care to make a third when they saw any two in Conversation."

Ironically, the *Bounty* arrived at the small island of Tubuai the same day that Bligh and his men arrived at Restoration Island, but unlike those set adrift, Christian had had plenty of time to plan for his arrival and he had made some unusual preparations at that. According to Morrison, "During this passage Mr. Christian Cut up the old Studding sails to make Uniforms for All hands, taking his own for edging, observing that nothing had more effect on the mind of the Indians as a uniformity of Dress, which by the by has its effect among Europeans as it always betokens discipline especially on board British Men of War."

Perhaps not surprisingly, the people of Tahiti were not as impressed with his "uniforms" as he had hoped they would be. Morrison reported, "When we got in with the Island the Small cutter was sent with Geo. Stuart to examine the reef, and find the Opening described by Captain Cook. While he was on this duty He was attacked by a number of the Natives in a Canoe who boarded him and Carried off a Jacket and some other things, Having no Arms but a brace of Pistols one of which missed fire, and they were not Certain that the other did execution, the Natives were armed with long spears which became useless at Close quarters by which means the boats Crew escaped being hurt and the natives being frightened by the report of the Pistol."

Given their less-than-friendly reception, the *Bounty* remained on Tubuai for only three days before leaving for Tahiti, where the crew arrived on June 6, 1789. At this point, Fletcher and the mutineers had to figure out what to tell the island's leaders, most of whom had met the men, and their lawful captain, just a few months earlier. The captain of the HMS *Pandora*, Edward Edwards, noted, "The Otoo and other natives were very inquisitive and desirous to know what was become of Lt. Bligh and the other absentees and the bread fruit plants, etc. They deceived them by saying that they had fallen in with Captain Cook at an island he had lately discovered called 'Why-Too-Tackee' [Aitutaki], and where he intended to settle, and that the plants were landed and planted there, and that Lt. Bligh and the other absentees were detained to assist Captain Cook in the business he had in hand, and that he had appointed Christian captain of the *Bounty* and ordered him to Otaheite for an additional supply of hogs, goats, fowls, bread fruit plants, etc. These humane islanders were imposed upon by this artful story, and they were so rejoiced to hear that their old friend Captain Cook was alive and was near them that they used every means in their power to procure the things that were wanted, so that in the course of a few days the *Bounty* took on board 312 hogs, 38 goats, eight dozen fowls, a bull and a cow, and a quantity of bread fruit plants. They also took with them a woman, eight men and seven boys."

With these supplies in hand, the men of the *Bounty* made their way back to Tubuai, hoping to establish a new settlement there.

Chapter 6: God Knows Whither

"Having anchored in Matavai bay, the next morning my messmate (Mr. Stewart) and I went on shore, to the house of an old landed proprietor, our former friend; and being now set free from a lawless crew, determined to remain as much apart from them as possible, and wait patiently for the arrival of a ship. Fourteen more of the Bounty's people came likewise on shore, and Mr. Christian and eight men went away with the ship, but God knows whither. Whilst we remained here, we were treated by our kind and friendly natives with a generosity and humanity almost unparalleled, and such as we could hardly have expected from the most civilized people." - Peter Heywood

It is difficult to say what was going through Fletcher Christian's mind during this time, but over the past 200 years, he has been depicted as everything from a determined visionary to a psychotic criminal. Given what is known of his life, chances are he was a little bit of both, but after taking the *Bounty* back to Tubuai, he proceeded to organize his men into settling the area as if it were a sanctioned colony, beginning with constructing a fort they named Fort George in honor of the English king, George III.

At first, it all seemed very comfortable and normal. Morrison remembered, "Measured out for the Fort possession was taken by turning a Turf and hoisting the Union Jack on a Staff in the Place. On this occasion an extra Allowance of Grog was drank and the Place Called Fort George, and finding the Place overrun with rats several Cats were brought on shore and let loose among them. ... Everything being settled, we proceeded to Work though not a man knew anything of Fortification; some Cut stakes others made Battens some Cut Sods and brought to hand, some built and others Wrought in the ditch, the Carpenters made barrows and Cut timber for the Gates and Drawbridge, and the work began to rise apace. Nor was Mr. Christian an Idle Spectator for He always took a part in the most laborious part of the Work, and half a Pint of Porter was served twice a day extra."

However, things soon went awry. After all, the men were mutineers and thus less inclined to work together under authority. The natives also continued to harass the men, compelling Morrison to consider finding somewhere else to live. He explained, "Mr. Christian now began to talk of taking the Masts out and dismantling the Ship when he intended to erect houses and live on shore, and as I had some hopes that I Could reach Tahiti in the large Cutter, I spoke to G. Stuart on the Affair, who told me that He and P. Heywood had formed the same plan; and as I knew that after the Masts were out I could put it out their power to get them in again by destroying the purchase Blocks and fall, and if we reached Tahiti were in no danger of being pursued I then advised him to get the Cutter repaired but He said Mr. Christian had said he would not Have the Boats repaired till he was on Shore; and to prevent any suspicion, we had better say nothing about it and was determined to take her as she was; and as We had some Reason to suppose that others were of the same way of thinking with ourselves we resolved to take the first Opportunity and provided accordingly, but Providence ordered things better and We had no need to make this rash attempt, though the passage was short and it might perhaps be made with safety in 5 or 6 days, yet had we the Chance to Meet with bad weather our Crazy boat would certainly have made us a Coffin which we did not now foresee."

In the end, Christian agreed that they should all return to Tahiti, where each man would make a life for himself in the best way he could. As a result, the *Bounty* sailed once more for Tahiti, where it arrived a few days later, but Christian himself did not stay there too long, probably due to his concerns about being arrested for mutiny. Instead, he and eight other mutineers boarded the *Bounty* once more and sailed away, this time with six Tahitian men, 11 women and an infant. On January 15, 1790, they arrived on Pitcairn Island, and in a bold act of commitment to staying there, they burned the *Bounty* on January 23, 1790. The mutineers did indeed found a settlement this time, and their descendants live there to this day, with January 23 still celebrated as "*Bounty* Day."

Meanwhile, the 16 men who remained on Tahiti intermarried with the native women, fathering children and eventually establishing a comfortable relationship with the people of the island. In time, they actually came to consider themselves Tahitians and later fought alongside their fellow islanders in battles to protect their homes. Indeed, they might have gone on to enjoy long and peaceful lives in their new homes had it not been for the man they had set adrift and who was determined to get back to England and report the dastardly deed: Captain William Bligh.

While the mutineers were trying to make new lives for themselves, Bligh was out to get his old life back. First, of course, he had to get back to civilization. Leaving Restoration Island, Bligh and his men set sail again to reach Coupang, in Timor. Bligh wrote, "At two o'clock this afternoon, having run through a very dangerous breaking sea, the cause of which I attributed to a strong tide setting to windward, and shoal water, we discovered a spacious bay or sound, with a fair entrance about two or three miles wide. I now conceived hopes that our voyage was nearly at an end, as no place could appear more eligible for shipping, or more likely to be chosen for an European settlement: I therefore came to a grapnel near the east side of the entrance, in a small sandy bay, where we saw a hut, a dog, and some cattle; and I immediately sent the boatswain and gunner away to the hut, to discover the inhabitants."

His next step was to obtain a new ship. On July 1, 1789, he purchased the *Resource* in Coupang, and he began putting together a crew. Using his credentials as an officer in the Royal Navy, he was able to recruit 17 men to sail with him, and after leaving Coupang on August 20, 1789, they made their way to Batavia. Once there, he was able to make arrangements to return to England: "It was, however, necessary for me to quit Batavia without delay; and the governor, on that account, gave me leave, with two others, to go in a packet that was to sail before the fleet; and assured me, that those who remained should be sent after me by the fleet, which was to sail before the end of the month: that if I remained, which would be highly hazardous, he could not send us all in one ship. My sailing, therefore, was eligible…and for that reason I embarked in the Vlydt packet, which sailed on the 16th of October. On the 16th of December, I arrived at the Cape of Good Hope, where I first observed that my usual health was returning; but for a long time I continued very weak and infirm. … On the 2d of January 1790, we sailed for Europe, and on the 14th of March, I was landed at Portsmouth by an Isle of Wight boat."

Once he was back in England, Bligh wasted no time in reporting the mutiny on March 16, 1790. He then turned his attention to writing his account of events, perhaps hoping to "tell the truth, tell it all, and tell it first." His narrative was published on July 1, 1790 and became very popular among readers of adventure stories, but Bligh's work was not done, for he still had to face a court martial as a result of having lost one of His Majesty's ships. On October 22, 1790, a brief hearing was held, and at the end, the Court ruled "that the said armed vessel, the *Bounty* was violently and forcibly taken from the said Lieutenant William Bligh by the said Fletcher Christian and certain other Mutineers, and did adjudge the said Lieutenant William Bligh, and such of the Officers and Ships Company as were returned to England and then present to be honorably acquitted." Thus, on November 14, 1790, Bligh was given a new command as captain of the HMS *Falcon*.

Chapter 7: Everything We Had Saved

"On the 31st the boats were completed and were launched, and we put everything we had saved on board of them and at half past ten in the forenoon we embarked, 30 on board the launch, 25 in the pinnace, 23 in one yawl and 21 in the other yawl. ... On the 1st September in the morning saw land, which probably was the continent of New South Wales. The yawls were sent on shore to ground and look out. They saw a run of water, landed and filled their two barricois, which were the only vessels of consequence they had with them, and I steered for an island called by Lt. Bligh Mountainous Island, and when joined by the boats ran into a bay of that island where we saw Indians on the beach. The water was shoal and the Indians waded off to the boats. ... They used many signs to signify that they wished us to land, but we declined their invitation from motives of prudence." - Captain Edward Edwards

As Bligh went through the process of clearing his name and getting a new commission, Captain Edward Edwards was ordered to track down the mutineers and bring them to justice, so he and his crew sailed from Portsmouth on November 7, 1790 on HMS *Pandora*. His orders were "to endeavor to recover the abovementioned Armed Vessel, and to bring in confinement to England the abovementioned Fletcher Christian and his Associates (a list of whose names you will receive herewith) or as many of them as have survived and you may be able to apprehend, in order that they may be brought to condign Punishment."

Edwards had no problems getting to Tahiti and arrived there on March 23, 1791, where he rounded up the mutineers that had remained on the island without incident. In fact, a number of them were anxious to give themselves up. Edwards noted, "Before we anchored at Matavy Bay, Joseph Coleman, Armorer of the *Bounty*, and several of the natives came on board, from whom I learned that Christian the pirate had landed and left 16 of his men on the Island, some of whom were then at Matavy, and some had sailed from there the morning before our arrival (in a schooner they had built) for Papara, a distant part of the Island, to join other of the pirates that were settled at that place, and that Churchill, Master at Arms, had been murdered by Matthew Thompson, and that Matthew Thompson was killed by the natives and offered as a sacrifice on their altars for the murder of Churchill, whom they had made a chief. George Stewart and Peter Heywood, midshipmen of the *Bounty*, came on board the Pandora soon after she came to an anchor, and I had also information that Richard Skinner was at Matavy. ... John Brown...from whom their Lordships supposed I might get some useful information, had been under the necessity for his own safety to associate with the pirates, but he took the opportunity to leave them when they were about to embark in the schooner and put to sea."

Having gathered the 14 remaining mutineers from the island, the *Pandora* left Tahiti on May 8, 1791 to continue their search for the *Bounty* and the rest of the deserters. During their search, the prisoners were housed in a cage Edwards humorously dubbed "Pandora's Box," but it soon became apparent that the trip home was not going to be an easy one. On May 24, just off of Palmerston Island, tragedy struck. Edwards had confiscated the mutineer's ship and brought it along with him as a tender, but according to his account, "During the night the weather was rougher than usual, with an ugly sea and I did not get close in with [the men sent out on the jolly boat] again till the 28th at noon, soon after which the yawl came on board from the schooner and informed us to my great astonishment and concern that the cutter had not been on board her since she left the ship. ... I then stood out to sea and the ship and the tender cruised about in search of the cutter until the 29th in the morning, when seeing nothing of her, I being at that time well in with the land, sent on shore once more to examine the reef and beach of the northernmost island, but with no better success than before, as neither the cutter or any article belonging to her could be found there."

In addition to the boat, Edwards lost five men, and about a month later, on June 22, tragedy struck again when the *Pandora* became separated from one of her tenders. Edwards searched for the missing ship and her nine crewmen for two days before giving them up for dead, but fortunately, the men survived and were eventually reunited with the rest of the crew in time to return with them to England.

Even still, the worst disaster was yet to come. On August 29, 1791, the *Pandora* wrecked itself running aground on the Great Barrier Reef. Edwards later wrote, "The ship struck upon the reef.... Got out the boats with a view to carrying out an anchor, but before it could be effected the ship struck so heavily on the reef that the carpenters reported that she made 18 inches of water in five minutes, and in five minutes after there was four feet of water in the hold. ... At this time the water only gained upon us in a small degree and we flattered ourselves for some time that by the assistance of a top sail which we were preparing and intended to haul under the ship's bottom we might be able to free her of water, but these flattering hopes did not continue long, for as she settled in the water the leaks increased and in so great a degree that there was reason to apprehend that she would sink before daylight. ... Our boats were kept astern of the ship; a small quantity of provisions and other necessaries were put into them, rafts were made, and all floating things upon the deck were unlashed. At half past six the hold was filled with water, and water was between decks and it also washed in at the upper deck ports, and there were strong indications that the ship was upon the very point of sinking, and we began to leap overboard and to take to the boats, and before everybody could get out of her the ship actually sank. The boats continued astern on the ship in the direction of the drift of the tide from here, and took up the people that had held on to the rafts or other floating things that had been cast loose for the purpose of supporting them in the water."

In spite of the captain's best efforts, he still lost a number of men. He continued, "We loaded two of the boats with people and sent them to the island, or rather key, about three or four miles from the ship, and then other two boats remained near the ship for some time and picked up all the people that could be seen and then followed the two first boats to the key, and after landing the people, the boats were immediately sent again to look about the wreck and the adjoining reefs for missing people, but they returned without having found a single person. On mustering we discovered that 89 of the ship's company and 10 of the pirates that were on board were saved, and that 31 of the ship's company and 4 pirates were lost with the ship."

An illustration depicting the sinking of the *Pandora*

To his credit, Edwards wasted no time getting the remaining men organized, and they were soon on their way again in the small boats they had saved. They made their way first to Coupang and then to Java, where he discovered the rest of his crew from the lost tender. According to David Renouard, a midshipman aboard the *Pandora*, "The very day after our arrival the *Rembang* Dutch Indiaman, put in here, having on board the remainder of the unfortunate Pandora's crew: thus a providential meeting took place no less joyful than unexpected. The pleasure that my late companions, in distress, must have felt, in again joining their old friends and shipmates, cannot be adequately expressed…The wary Dutchmen at length convinced that we were no imposters, gave us up with the Tender to Captain Edwards…."

On June 18, 1792, after their long ordeal, the crew of the Pandora finally arrived in England with their 10 prisoners. Edwards' trials and tribulations were over, but those of the mutineers were just beginning.

Chapter 8: Shall Suffer Death

"Every person in or belonging to the fleet, who shall desert or entice others so to do, shall suffer death, or such other punishment as the circumstances of the offense shall deserve, and a court martial shall judge fit: and if any commanding officer of any of His Majesty's ships or vessels of war shall receive or entertain a deserter from any other of His Majesty's ships or vessels, after discovering him to be such deserter, and shall not with all convenient speed give notice to the captain of the ship or vessel to which such deserter belongs; or if the said ships or vessels are at any considerable distance from each other, to the secretary of the admiralty, or to the commander in chief; every person so offending, and being convicted thereof by the sentence of the court martial, shall be cashiered." - Article 16 of the Articles of War "established from the 25th of December 1749; and…directed to be observed and put in execution, as well in time of peace as in time of war."

On September 12, 1792, a military tribunal assembled aboard HMS *Duke* in Portsmouth. The Right Honorable Lord Hood presided over the court and appears to have done a remarkably good job in running a fair hearing, especially considering the time and circumstances.

John Fryer testified first, speaking in colorful terms about every detail of the mutiny. He was then questioned by James Morrison, Michael Byrn, Thomas Burkitt and John Millward, all of whom were acting in their own defense. William Cole testified next and was also duly cross examined. Next, William Purcell was called to the stand, but by this time, the court seemed to be particularly interested in Heywood's involvement in the mutiny. Purcell was asked to "[r]elate to the Court all you know of Mr. Heywood's Conduct on that Day from the beginning of the Mutiny until you left the Ship?" Purcell answered, "When I came upon Deck he was in his Berth; I did not see him on Deck until the Launch was ordered to be hoisted out, when he was standing on the Booms resting his Hand on a Cutlass—I exclaimed, 'in the Name of God, Peter, what do you do with that!' when he instantly dropped it and assisted in hoisting the Launch out and handing the Things into the Boat, my Chest and all the other Articles, and then went down below, when I heard Churchill call to Thompson to keep them below, but could not tell whom he meant. I did not see Mr. Heywood after that."

Fryer

He was asked similarly about Michael Byrn and replied, "The first thing I observed of him was his being in the large Cutter to keep her from the side, in which Situation he remained when we left the Ship, but was crying and said if he was with us he could be of no manner of Service to us—he being Blind; he was not Armed." However, when asked about Ellison he was very clear, saying, "When I came on Deck, he was standing near the Gangway on the Larboard Side, Armed with a Musket and Bayonet; in that Situation he was during the whole time to the best of my Knowledge in different parts of the Ship."

On the other hand, Purcell's testimony about Millward was less damning: "When I came on Deck Millward was one of those People that were in their Hammocks, which Mr. Cole turned up; when he came on the Booms he said, 'Mr. Purcell, I assure you I know nothing Of this Business, but as I had a hand in the former foolish Affair I suppose they will oblige me, or force me,'—I can't positively say which—'to take a part in this.' I saw Millward afterwards down the after Ladder by Mr. Fryer's Cabin Armed with a Musquet, but don't recollect his having a Bayonet fixed in it; I don't recollect seeing him afterwards until we were in the Boat, when I saw him look over the Taffrail but can't tell whether he was Armed or not."

After a few other crewmen from the *Bounty* testified, Edwards was called to share his impressions of the men when he picked them up in Tahiti. He noted, "Joseph Coleman attempted to come on board before the Ship came to an Anchor at Otaheite— he was soon afterwards taken up by Canoes, and came on board before the Ship came to an Anchor. I began to make Enquiries of him after the "*Bounty*" and her People. He informed us that some of the People were at a Place Called Mativy, near the Place where the Ship Anchored at, and the others had sailed from Mativy in a Schooner that had been built by the "*Bounty*'s" People; … To the best of my recollection he seemed to be ready to give me any Information that I asked of him. The next who came on board, were Stewart and Peter Heywood…Peter Heywood I think said he supposed I had heard of the Affair of the "*Bounty*." I don't recollect all the Conversation that passed between us; he sometimes interrupted me by asking for Mr. Hayward, the Lieutenant of the 'Pandora,' whether he was on Board or not; he had heard that he was; at last I acknowledged that he was, and I desired him to come out of my Stateroom, where I had desired him to go into, as he happened to be with me at the time. Lieutenant Hayward treated him with a sort of contemptuous look, and began to enter into Conversation with him respecting the '*Bounty*,' but I called the Sentinel in to take them into Custody, and ordered Lieutenant Hayward to desist, and I ordered them to be put into Irons; some Words passed and Peter Heywood said he hoped he should be able to vindicate his Conduct."

Edwards was the last substantial witness for the prosecution, which rested its case on September 14. The following day, the accused began to defend themselves, calling forth their former friends to offer some sort of testimony that might save their lives and offering their own defenses of their actions. John Millwood, the last of the men to offer any defense, completed his testimony on Monday, September 17, 1792.

The court handed down its verdict the following day: "That the Charges had been proved against the said Peter Heywood, James Morrison, Thomas Ellison, Thomas Burkitt, John Millward and William Muspratt, and did adjudge them and each of them to suffer Death by being hanged by the Neck, on board such of His Majesty's Ship or Ships of War, at such Time or Times and at such Place or Places, as the Commissioners for executing the Office of Lord High Admiral of Great Britain and Ireland etc. or any three of them, for the Time being, should in Writing, under their Hands direct; but the Court, in Consideration of various Circumstances, did humbly and most earnestly recommend the said Peter Heywood and James Morrison to His Majesty's Royal Mercy—and the Court further agreed That the Charges had not been proved against the said Charles Norman, Joseph Coleman, Thomas McIntosh and Michael Byrn, and did adjudge them and each of them to be acquitted."

Fortunately for them, Heywood and Morrison were indeed pardoned and enjoyed uneventful lives. Likewise, Muspratt's conviction was overturned with the help of his attorney, Stephen Barney, who submitted the following written objection on behalf of his client at the close of the hearing: "I have not the most distant Idea of arraigning the Justice of the Court, but I have to lament that the Practice and usage of a Court Martial, should be so different from the Practice of all Criminal Courts of Justice on Shore, as that, by the one I have been debarred calling Witnesses whose Evidence I have Reason to believe, would have tended to have proved my Innocence, whereas by the other I should have been permitted to call those very Witnesses on my behalf. This Difference, my Lord, is dreadful to the Subject and fatal to me."

The court reviewed the case and overturned Muspratt's conviction, but Ellison, Burkitt, and

Millward were not so fortunate. On October 29, 1792, according to the log of HMS *Brunswick*, "At 5 [AM] Received 3 Prisoners from the Hector, Namely John Milward, Thomas Ellison, and Thomas Burkitt...At 9 [AM] Fired a gun and made the Signal for Boats, Manned and Armed, at 26 Past 11 Fired a gun as Signal for Execution when Thomas Burkitt was Run up to the Starboard Fore Yard Arm, Milward and Ellison to the Larboard, and There Hung Agreeable to their Sentence per Court Martial for Mutiny On Board the *Bounty*, Captain Blyth, on Return from Otahaita."

If in their final moments any of the three executed that day felt it was unfair that they were caught and Christian escaped, they need not have fretted, because the man who could not follow his captain could not lead either, and he soon lost control of his new home on Pitcairn. A rebellion started between he and his men in the summer of 1793, and Christian died in the ensuing fighting on September 20, 1793, along with five more other mutineers. Thus, he who chose to live by the sword did indeed die by the sword.

The *Amistad*

Chapter 1: The Amistad's Journey

"The Africans of the Amistad were cast upon our coast in a condition perhaps as calamitous as could befall human beings, not by their own will - not with any intention hostile or predatory on their part, not even by the act of God as in the case of shipwreck, but by their own ignorance of navigation and the deception of one of their oppressors whom they had overpowered, and whose life they had spared to enable them by his knowledge of navigation to reach their native land. They were victims of the African slave trade, recently imported into the island of Cuba, in gross violation of the laws of the Island and of Spain; and by acts which our own laws have made piracy - punishable with death. They had indicated their natural right to liberty, by conspiracy, insurrection, homicide and capture and they were accused by the two Cuban Spaniards embarked with them in the ship, of murder and piracy - and they were claimed by the same two Cuban Spaniards, accessories after the fact to the slave-trade piracy, by which they had been brought from Africa to Cuba, as their property, because they had bought them from slave-trade pirates." John Quincy Adams in a letter written in November 1839

The legend of the *Amistad* began in June 1839, when a group of young men were captured illegally in Africa and were set to be transported against their will to Havana, Cuba. Given the ban on the slave trade, the completely illegal nature of their capture would prove to be an integral part of the court case that would make them, and their captors, famous. Congressman Joshua Reed Giddings, an ardent abolitionist, spelled out some of the background in the trial that followed: "[A]s early as 1817 Spain took upon herself the most solemn obligations to abolish this slave trade...In perfect good faith, the Crown of Spain, by its decadal order, issued soon after, declared the slave trade abolished throughout her dominions, including her colonial possessions; and asserted the freedom of all Africans who should be thereafter imported into any of her national or colonial ports…[C]ertain Cuban slave dealers continued to violate the laws and treaties of their own Government, the rights of human nature, and the laws of God, by importing and enslaving the unoffending people of Africa. In 1839 they imported a cargo of these inoffensive victims to Havana, in the Island of Cuba…[T]hey were seized in Africa about the middle of April 1839, force carried on board the slave ship, and on the 12th June of that year they were landed in Havana, and imprisoned in the barracoons of that city."

Giddings

Shortly after the Africans landed in Havana, they were purchased by two Spanish citizens, Jose Ruiz and Pedro Montes, who planned to sell the slaves to plantation owners elsewhere on the island. As a result, a ship called *La Amistad* ("The Friendship") left Havana to travel to the province of Puerto Principe, also located on the island of Cuba. At that time, Cuba was still a Spanish colony.

A replica of the *Amistad* is now docked at Mystic Seaport, Connecticut, home of the largest maritime museum in the world.

The ship was under the command of Captain Ramón Ferrer, with Ruiz and Montes serving as crew and a cook onboard. The ship's "cargo" consisted of 53 Africans being sent by the governor-general of Cuba to Puerto Principe, but there was a problem with his plan for them. As Giddings later explained, "These Africans were in no way parties to these permits, knew nothing of their being granted; and I need say their rights could not be affected in any way by them…they were in no respect admissible evidence against the Negroes, who had been imported in fraud, and in violation of Spanish treaties and Spanish laws."

More problems arose when the crew ran out of food and water five days into what was supposed to be a four-day voyage. Naturally, the ship's crew decided to keep what little provisions that were left for themselves, leaving the poor Africans to starve. Some of the Africans would later claim that the cook, a man named Celestino, admitted to them that the crew might eventually resort to killing the Africans themselves for food.

Ultimately, the captives decided to take their chances with a mutiny and to die as free men rather than live as slaves. Thus, as Giddings continued, "On the 1st day of July, while sailing along the eastern coast of the Island, the Africans rose and claimed their freedom. The captain and cook attempted to reduce them to subjection, and were slain; Montes and Ruiz, and the two sailors, surrendered the ship [to the] Africans. They immediately sent the sailors to shore in the boat, and retaining Montes and Ruiz on board, directed them to steer the ship for Africa. But, during the darkness of the night, they directed their course northwardly, and on the 26th of August, being sixty days from the time of leaving Havana, they came to anchor off the Connecticut coast, near the eastern shore of Long Island. While the vessel was thus riding at anchor, Lieutenant Gedney, of the ship Washington, engaged in the coast survey of the United States, took possession of her, and of the cargo and people on board, and carried them into the port of New London."

The leader of the mutineers was a young man, Sengbe Pieh, who later became known as Joseph Cinqué. Cinqué was able to escape his own bonds by using a file that had been given to him by a woman during their trip from Africa to Cuba, and he then freed the other captives. In addition to the captain and the cook, two of the Africans lost their lives during the skirmish.

1840 portrait of Cinqué

A sketch depicting Cinqué in traditional Muslim garb

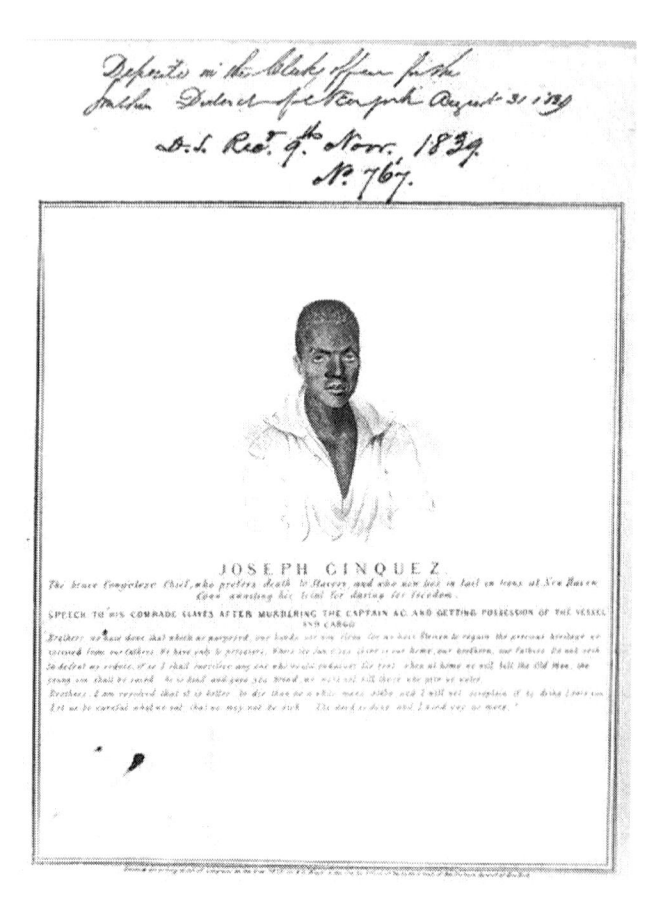

A depiction of Cinqué that appeared in a New York newspaper, *The Sun*, in August 1839

Thus, even though the Africans had successfully overrun the crew, their lack of nautical knowledge allowed the ship to be captured when it arrived at Culloden Point on Long Island on August 26, 1839. There was some misunderstanding as to when exactly the ship arrived in New York, with some records indicating that it was not until August 1840, but it's doubtful that the ship was at sea for over a year traveling from Cuba to New York. Furthermore, the *New London Gazette* reported the *Amistad*'s story on August 26, 1839, and in doing so, the paper presented a clearly biased account of how the ship arrived there:

> "While this vessel was sounding this day between Gardner's and Montauk Points, a schooner was seen lying in shore off Culloden Point, under circumstances so

suspicious as to authorize Lt. Com. Gedney to stand in to see what was her character--seeing a number of people on the beach with carts and horses, and a boat passing to and fro a boat was armed and dispached with an officer to board her. On coming along side a number of negroes were discovered on her deck, and twenty or thirty more were on the beach--two white men came forward and claimed the protection of the officer. The schooner proved to be the "Amistad," Capt. Ramonflues, from the Havana bound to Guanaja, Port Principe, with 54 blacks and two passengers on board

    The situation of the two whites was all this time truly deplorable, being treated with the greatest severity, and Pedro Montes, who had charge of the navigation, was suffering from two severe wounds, one in the head and one in the arm, their lives threatened every instant. He was ordered to change the course again for the coast of Africa, the negroes themselves steering by the sun in the day time, while at night he would alter their course so as to bring them back to their original place of destination.--They remained three days off Long Island, to the Eastward of Providence, after which time they were two months on the ocean, sometimes steering to the Eastward, and whenever an occasson [sic] would permit the whites would alter the course to the Northward and Westward, always in hopes of falling in with some vessel of war, or being enabled to run into some port, when they would be relieved from their horrid situation.

    Several times they were boarded by vessels; once by an American schooner from Kingston. On these occasions the whites were ordered below, while the negroes communicated and traded with the vessel; the schooner from Kingston supplied them with a demijohn of water, for the moderate sum of one doubloon--this schooner, whose name was not ascertained, finding that the negroes had plenty of money, remained lashed alongside the "Amistad" for twenty-four hours, though they must have been aware that all was not right on board, and probably suspected the character of the vessel--that was on the 18th of the present month; the vessel was steered to the northward and westward, and on the 20th instant, distant from N.Y. 25 miles, the pilot boat No. 3 came alongside and gave the negroes some apples. She was also hailed by No. 4; when the latter boat came near, the negroes armed themselves and would not permit her to board them; they were so exasperated with the two whites for bringing them so much out of their way that they expected every moment to be murdered."

When some of the men left the ship to go ashore for food and water, the USS *Washington* spotted the ship, which they had been told was stolen. Lieutenant Thomas R. Gedney, then in command of the *Washington*, captured the ship and those aboard, and he subsequently sailed the ship to New London, Connecticut, where slavery was legal.

People in town quickly heard of the ship's arrival and the story of what supposedly happened aboard it, all of which made good grist for sensationalist accounts. A reporter sent to investigate later wrote, "On board the brig we also saw Cinqué, the master spirit and hero of this bloody tragedy, in irons. He is about five feet eight inches in height, 25 or 26 years of age, of erect figure, well built, and very active. He is said to be a match for any two men aboard the schooner. His countenance, for a native African, is unusually intelligent, evincing uncommon decision and coolness, with a composure characteristic of true courage, and nothing to mark him a malicious man. ... On her deck were grouped amid various goods and arms, the remnant of her Ethiopian crew, some decked in the most fantastic manner, in silks and finery, pilfered from the cargo, while others, in a state of nudity, emaciated to mere skeletons, lay coiled upon the decks. ... On the forward hatch we unconsciously rested our hand on a cold object, which we soon discovered to be a naked corpse, enveloped in a pall of black bombazine. On removing its folds, we beheld the rigid countenance and glazed eye of a poor Negro who died last night. His mouth was unclosed and still wore the ghastly expression of his last struggle."

A contemporary portrait of one of the Africans on the *Amistad*

Chapter 2: Under What Authority

"I do not, in fact, understand how a foreign court of justice can be considered competent to take cognizance of an offence committed on board of a Spanish vessel, by Spanish subjects, and against Spanish subjects, in the waters of a Spanish territory; for it was committed on the coasts of this island, and under the flag of this nation." - Cavallero Pedro Alcantara Argaiz, Spanish minister

The matter first came before the courts when Montes and Ruiz tried to claim ownership of the Africans. According to court transcripts, "On the 29th of August, 1839 — being precisely two months and one day from the time of leaving the port of Havana — Montes and Ruiz filed their claim in the district court of the United States, demanding these Africans as their slaves. On the 19th September, 1839, the Africans filed their answers to claim of Montes and Ruiz ... denying that they were, or ever had been, slaves to Montes and Ruiz, or to any other person; but that they were, and ever had been, free."

Making the matter even more complex, Montes and Ruiz were not the only ones who felt that they had a right to claim ownership of the "cargo," because Gedney also claimed ownership based on the laws of salvage. Connecticut Judge James Dixon explained, "The vessel, with the Negroes on board, having been brought by Lieutenant Gedney into the district of Connecticut, was there, by him, libeled for salvage in the district court of the United States. A libel for salvage was also filed by other parties, who claimed to have aided in saving the ship by arresting the Negroes on shore."

Furthermore, the others mentioned as claiming rights to the Africans included "Henry Green and Pelatiah Fordham and others, [who] filed a petition and answer to the libel, claiming salvage out of the property proceeded against by Thomas R. Gedney and others, and stating, that before the *Amistad* was seen or boarded by the officers and crew of the Washington, they had secured a portion of the Negroes who had come on shore, and had thus aided in saving the vessel and cargo." Even the Spanish government became involved when "[o]n the 19th of September, the district attorney of the United States for the district of Connecticut filed an information, or libel, setting forth the claim of the Spanish Government under the treaty of 1795, renewed in 1821."

Up to this point, the case was not that unique, as maritime cases related to salvage came through the courts on a regular basis during the 19th century. However, the new wrinkle appeared when the Africans, with the help of several sympathetic American attorneys, filed a claim to their own freedom: "To these various libels, the Negroes, Cinqué and others ... on the 7th of January, 1840, filed an answer, denying that they were slaves or the property of Ruiz and Montes, or that the court could ... exercise any jurisdiction over their persons, by reason of the premises; and praying that they might be dismissed. They specially set forth and insisted, that they were native-born Africans; that they were born free, and still of right ought to be free, and not slaves; that they were, on or about the 15th day of April, 1839, unlawfully kidnapped and forcibly and wrongfully carried on board a certain vessel, on the coast of Africa, which was unlawfully engaged in the slave trade, and were unlawfully transported in the same vessel to the

Island of Cuba, for the purpose of being unlawfully sold as slaves; that Ruiz and Montes ... made a pretended purchase of them, that afterwards ... caused them, without law or right, to be placed on board the said *Amistad*, to be transported to some place unknown to them, to be enslaved for life; that on the voyage they rose and took possession of the vessel, intending to return therewith to their native country, or to seek an asylum in some free State."

Of course, the Africans were at a distinct disadvantage when it came to defending themselves against this action, which Giddings later pointed out: "Here I will remark that the Africans were strangers in a strange land, ignorant of any language save their native dialect — without friends, without influence, and without money. One would have reasonably supposed that the sympathies of all men and all Government officers would have been enlisted in favor of these persecuted exiles, who had been thus torn from their homes, their country, their kindred and friends. The dictates of our nature are in favor of the oppressed, the friendless, of those who are incapable of defending their own rights." However, as the case became public and federal leaders became involved, Giddings ruefully noted, "Yet I feel humbled, as an American, when I say that the President [Martin Van Buren] sent orders to the United States Attorney for the district of Connecticut, directing him to appear before the court, and in the name of the Spanish Minister to demand these Africans, in order that they may be delivered over to their pretended owners." Of course, Van Buren, who was seeking reelection in 1840, was much more concerned about the Southern slave owners whose votes he needed than appeasing the Spanish, but it did throw another angle into the already complicated case.

Van Buren

Chapter 3: Mutiny and Murder?

A page from a deposition in the mutiny case against the Africans

"Great Britain is also bound to remember that the law of Spain, which finally prohibited the slave-trade throughout the Spanish dominions, from the date of the 30th of May, 1820, the provisions of which law are contained in the King of Spain's royal cedula of the 19th December, was passed, in compliance with a treaty obligation to that effect, by which the Crown of Spain had bound itself to the Crown of Great Britain, and for which a valuable compensation, in return, was given by Great Britain to Spain; as may be seen by reference to the 2d, 3d, and 4th articles of a public treaty concluded between Great Britain and Spain on the 23d of September, 1817." – Henry Stephen Fox, British diplomat

Even as the civil case was ongoing to determine who if anyone owned the Africans, a case charging them with mutiny and murder commenced, and the first hearing was held aboard the *Washington* while most of the Africans were confined in a jail in New Haven, Connecticut. Beginning on August 29, Judge Andrew T. Judson heard charges and testimony concerning the 39 Africans accused of murdering the captain and the cook. During the trial, Ruiz testified, "I took an oar and tried to quell the mutiny. I cried 'No! No!' I then heard one of the crew cry murder. I then heard the captain order the cabin boy to go below and get some bread to throw among the Negroes, hoping to pacify them. I did not see the captain killed." Next, Montes added his testimony, saying that on the fourth night that the ship was out to sea, "[b]etween three and four [I] was awakened by a noise which was caused by blows to the mulatto cook. I went on deck and they attacked me. I seized a stick and a knife with a view to defend myself...At this time [Cinqué] wounded me on the head severely with one of the sugar knives, also on the arm. I then ran below and stowed myself between two barrels, wrapped up in a sail. [Cinqué] rushed after me and attempted to kill me, but was prevented by the interference of another man...I was then taken on deck and tied to the hand of Ruiz."

Following this hearing, Judson bound the case over to trial in a Connecticut circuit court, a federal court. Meanwhile, the Africans remained in custody, though they were apparently well treated and allowed a great deal of freedom to move about and be comfortable. The jailors seemed to have taken a liking to the children in the group and occasionally arranged for them to take rides in a wagon around the grounds. During this time, the Africans became a source of public curiosity and were seen by many in a very sympathetic light.

Perhaps concerned about the sympathy the Africans were receiving, Ruiz and Montes decided to go to work on public opinion. On the afternoon of the hearing, the following appeared in the New London newspaper: "The subscribers, Don Jose Ruiz, and Don Pedro Montes, in gratitude for their most unhoped for and providential rescue from the bands of a ruthless gang of African buccaneers and an awful death, would take the means of expressing, in some slight decree, their thankfulness and obligation to Lieut. Com T. R. Gedney, and the officers and crew of the U. S surveying brig Washington, for their decision in seizing the *Amistad*, and their unremitting kindness and hospitality in providing for their comfort on board their vessel, as well as the means they have taken for the protection of their property. We also must express our indebtedness to that nation whose flag they so worthily bear, with an assurance that the act will be duly appreciated by our most gracious sovereign, her Majesty the Queen of Spain."

Meanwhile, an abolitionist named Lewis Tappan banded with some of his fellow abolitionists to create the Friend of Amistad Africans Committee, and he then traveled to New Haven to meet the men he hoped to befriend in person. It was there he learned that the Africans were from the Mende tribe in Africa, and with that knowledge, he was able to secure a translator who would allow him to communicate with them. Tappan wrote, "I arrived here last Friday evening, with three men who are natives of Africa…to act as interpreters in conversing with Joseph Cinqué and his comrades. ... You may imagine the joy manifested by these poor Africans, when they heard one of their own color address them in a friendly manner, and in a language they could comprehend! ... I have read an ingenious and well written article in the Evening Post signed Veto, in which the learned writer presents a pretty full examination of the case of the schooner *Amistad*... [W]here there exists no treaty stipulation, as there does not at present between the United States and Spain...this country ought not to surrender persons situated as are Joseph Cinqué and his unfortunate countrymen, who are, by the act of God, thrown upon these shores to find, I trust, that protection and relief of which they had been, probably, forever deprived had it not been for this remarkable and providential interposition."

Lewis Tappan

The Africans may have gained a measure of relief from meeting Tappan and an interpreter, but their fates very much hung in the balance, and on September 6, Calderon de la Barca wrote to the American Secretary of State, John Forsyth, on behalf of the Spanish government. De la Barca made the following demands:

"1st. That the vessel be immediately delivered up to her owner, together with every article found on board at the time of her capture by the Washington, without any payment being exacted on the score of salvage, nor any charges made, other than those specified in the treaty of 1795, article 1st.

2d. That it be declared that no tribunal in the United States has the right to institute proceedings against, or to impose penalties upon, the subjects of Spain, for crimes committed on board a Spanish vessel, and in the waters of the Spanish territory.

3d. That the Negroes be conveyed to Havana, or be placed at the disposal of the proper authorities in that part of Her Majesty's dominions, in order to their being tried by the Spanish laws which they have violated; and that, in the meantime, they be kept in safe custody, in order to prevent their evasion.

4th. That if, in consequence of the intervention of the authorities of Connecticut, there should be any delay in the desired delivery of the vessel and the slaves, the owners both of the latter and of the former be indemnified for the injury that may accrue to them."

De la Barca then added, for good measure, what might be construed as a veiled threat: "In support of these claims, the undersigned invokes the law of nations, the stipulations of existing treaties, and those good feelings so necessary to the maintenance of the friendly relations that subsist between the two countries, and are so interesting to both".

Secretary of State Forsyth

The following week, on September 14, 1839, U.S. Supreme Court Justice Smith Thompson, who had convened the lower circuit court, heard requests from a federal attorney requesting that the Africans be turned over to President Van Buren for return to Cuba. Thompson decided that since the mutiny took place in international waters, American courts had no jurisdiction over the charges against the Africans. However, Thompson sent the civil case to the U.S. District Court for the District Court of Connecticut to decide who had ownership of the Africans on the *Amistad*.

Smith Thompson

In October 1839, with the help of Tappan and other members of the Friends committee, Cinqué and the other Africans filed charges against Ruiz and Montes for assault and false imprisonment. The two were arrested, and Montes quickly decided that he no longer had any interest in his "property," so he posted bail and boarded the first ship he could back to Cuba. Ruiz, on the other hand, found American jail enough to his liking that he decided to remain in the United States and stand trial. However, this situation did not last for long, as he too soon posted bail and returned to Cuba. As Iyunolu Folayan Osagie, author of *The Amistad Revolt: Memory, Slavery, and the Politics of Identity in the United States and Sierra Leone*, put it, Ruiz was "more comfortable in a New England setting (and entitled to many amenities not available to the Africans), [and] hoped to garner further public support by staying in jail...Ruiz, however, soon tired of his martyred lifestyle in jail and posted bond. Like Montez, he returned to Cuba".

Montes and Ruiz may have decided the trouble wasn't worth pursuing a case, but the Spanish government was furious that their citizens had been arrested in the first place. The Spanish ambassador, Cavallero Pedro Alcantara Argaiz, took a personal interest in the situation and demanded that the entire case related to the *Amistad* be thrown out of court. Furthermore, he insisted that the bail money the men posted be returned to them since "by the treaty of 1795, no obstacle or impediment" should have kept them from leaving.

However, the fact that Montes and Ruiz were indeed allowed to leave the United States was later used by the Africans' attorneys in their argument on behalf of the Africans' freedom: "Now, sir, when the *Amistad* came within our jurisdiction, when our laws spread their aegis over the people on board, it was a matter of course that those people were as free to go where they pleased, as were Montes and Ruiz. Indeed, those Spaniards were themselves restored to liberty by the force of our laws; and the Negroes, had they been held as legal slaves in Cuba, under Spanish laws, would have been as free, the moment they came within our jurisdiction, as were Montes and Ruiz."

Chapter 4: Unfortunate Under Such Circumstances

The wheels of justice slowed with the coming of winter; in November, the U.S. District Court for the District of Connecticut met to review the case but then chose to postpone trying it. Thus, they did not get around to hearing evidence until January 8, 1840, when the civil trial began in New Haven. The abolitionists spoke first, putting forth the argument that since Spain had made it illegal to capture and transport slaves to the United States in 1817, the Africans could not be legally owned by anyone but instead had been kidnapped. Therefore, they should be allowed to return to Africa. They also accused the Cuban government, and by extension the government of Spain, of falsifying documents to make it appear that the Africans in question had actually been born on the island.

On January 10, an American attorney, W. S. Holabird, countered the abolitionists' assertions while appearing in court on behalf of Spain's attorney (A.G. Vega). Holabird asserted, "That [Vega] is a Spanish subject; that he resided in the island of Cuba several years; that he knows the laws of that island on the subject of slavery; that there was no law that was considered in force in the island of Cuba, that prohibited the bringing in African slaves; that the court of mixed commissioners had no jurisdiction, except in cases of capture on the sea; that newly-imported African Negroes were constantly brought to the island, and after landing, were bon a fide transferred from one owner to another, without any interference by the local authorities or the mixed commission, and were held by the owners, and recognized as lawful property; that slavery was recognized in Cuba, by all the laws that were considered in force there; that the native language of the slaves was kept up on some plantations, for years. That the barracoons are public markets, where all descriptions of slaves are sold and bought; that the papers of the *Amistad* are genuine, and are in the usual form; that it was not necessary to practice any fraud, to obtain such papers from the proper officers of the government…"

On January 15, Judge Andrew Judson, on behalf of the court, ruled in favor of the Africans and ordered the President of the United States to return them to their homeland. However, Van Buren refused to carry out the court's order and instead instructed Holabird to file an appeal with the U.S. Circuit Court for the Connecticut District. The notion that the American president was not just advocating Spanish interests but actually directing Spain's legal course of action appalled many citizens in and around Connecticut and led the editor of the *Hartford Courant* to publish the following scathing editorial on February 10, 1840: "We are informed Martin Van Buren addressed a letter to the Judge recommending and urging him to order the Africans to be taken back to Havana in a government vessel, to be sold there as slaves…The letter of the President, recommending that these poor unfortunate Africans be sent into perpetual bondage, is said to contain statements disgraceful to the high station of its author, and which, were they published, would excite the indignation of every Republican freeman in the land. What will the friends of liberty say to this? Surely Martin Van Buren is playing the part of a tyrant with a high hand - else why this tampering with our courts of justice, this Executive usurpation, and this heartless violation of the inalienable rights of man? Of the truth of the above there is no doubt, and we leave the unprincipled author of such a proceeding in the hands of a just and high-minded People."

In April 1840, the United States Senate also weighed in on the case. Under the leadership of Southern statesman John C. Calhoun, the members voted to issue two resolutions that they hoped might guide the courts:

> "1. Resolved—That a ship or vessel on the high seas, in time of peace, engaged in a lawful voyage, is according to the laws of nations under the exclusive jurisdiction of the state to which her flag belongs as much as if constituting a part of its own domain.
>
> 2. Resolved—That if such ship or vessel should be forced, by stress of weather, or other unavoidable cause into the port, and under the jurisdiction of a friendly power, she and her cargo, and persons on board, with their property, and all the rights belonging to their personal relations, as established by the laws of the state to which they belong, would be placed under the protection which the laws of nations extend to the unfortunate under such circumstances."

Ironically, these resolutions were later cited not by those working against the Africans' freedom but by those in favor of it.

Chapter 5: Supreme Arguments

"This review of all the proceedings of the Executive I have made with utmost pain, because it was necessary to bring it fully before your Honors, to show that the course of that department had been dictated, throughout, not by justice but by sympathy – and a sympathy the most partial and injust. And this sympathy prevailed to such a degree, among all the persons concerned in this business, as to have perverted their minds with regard to all the most sacred principles of law and right, on which the liberties of the United States are founded; and a course was pursued, from the beginning to the end, which was not only an outrage upon the persons whose lives and liberties were at stake, but hostile to the power and independence of the judiciary itself." – John Quincy Adams

In August 1840, the African prisoners were transferred from cells in New Haven to Westville, a New Haven suburb, where they received an esteemed visitor: Congressman John Quincy Adams, son of the second president of the United States and a former president in his own right. Of all the causes that Quincy Adams championed during the final years of his life, none was as dear to his heart as ending slavery. In fact, in order to bring the issue into public debate, he brought to the floor of the United States House of Representatives a petition for the New England states to secede from the Union if the institution of slavery remained legal. Though he claimed his petition was merely meant to get the debate rolling, his fellow Congressmen were enraged by his actions.

In response to his action, his political opponents called for his censure, and he was tried for two long weeks. Unconcerned about a possible conviction, he used the debates not to defend himself but to castigate slave owners and their representatives in Congress, singling out future presidential candidate Stephen Douglas for his particular ire. He also scolded Congress for the "gag rule" that kept the debate over slavery from being addressed directly in Congressional debates. While the rule remained unchanged, so did Quincy Adams. In 1838, he wrote to a friend, "The conflict between the principle of liberty and the fact of slavery is coming gradually to an issue. Slavery has now the power, and falls into convulsions at the approach of freedom. That the fall of slavery is predetermined in the counsels of Omnipotence I cannot doubt; it is a part of the great moral improvement in the condition of man, attested by all the records of history. But the conflict will be terrible, and the progress of improvement perhaps retrograde before its final progress to consummation."

John Quincy Adams

After Quincy Adams visited the men, he offered to represent them before the U.S. Circuit Court of the Connecticut District, and due in part to his excellent arguments, the U.S. Circuit Court upheld the District Court's decision in September 1840.

Still unwilling to give up, Van Buren ordered the case appealed to the United States Supreme Court, and that court opened its session on February 23, 1841 with oral arguments from Attorney General Henry D. Gilpin. Gilpin was a Van Buren appointee and owed his career to the goodwill of the president, so he was fully committed to winning the case.

In the argument, Gilpin stated:

> "[T]he minister of Spain demands that the vessel, cargo, and Negroes, be restored, pursuant to the 9th article of the treaty of 27th October, 1795, which provides that 'all ships and merchandise of what nature whatsoever, which shall be rescued out of the hands of any pirates or robbers, on the high seas, shall be brought into some port of either state, and shall be delivered into the custody of the officers of that port, in order to be taken care of and restored entire to the true proprietor, as soon as due and sufficient proof shall be made concerning the property thereof.'

The only inquiries, then, that present themselves, are,

1. Has 'due and sufficient proof concerning the property thereof' been made?

2. If so, have the United States a right to interpose in the manner they have done, to obtain its restoration to the Spanish owners?

If these inquiries result in the affirmative, then the decree of the Circuit Court was erroneous, and ought to be reversed."

In answering the questions he had just posed, Gilpin set forth a number of arguments:

"It is submitted that there has been due and sufficient proof concerning the property to authorize its restoration.

It is not denied that, under the laws of Spain, Negroes may be held as slaves, ... nor will it be denied, if duly proved to be such, they are subject to restoration as much as other property, when coming under the provisions of this treaty. Now these Negroes are declared, by the certificates of the Governor General, to be slaves, and the property of the Spanish subjects ... the highest functionary of the government in Cuba; his public acts are the highest evidence of any facts stated by him, within the scope of his authority. It is within the scope of his authority to declare what is property, and what are the rights of the subjects of Spain, within his jurisdiction, in regard to property.

Now, in the intercourse of nations, there is no rule better established than this: that full faith is to be given to such acts -- to the authentic evidence of such acts. The question is not whether the act is right or wrong; it is, whether the scope of what had been done, and whether it is an act within the scope of the authority. We are to inquire only whether the power existed, and whether it was exercised, and how it was exercised; not whether it was rightly or wrongly exercised."

The glaring hole in Gilpin's argument was that significant evidence indicated that the Governor General of Cuba was wrong (either knowingly or unknowingly) about the validity of the Africans' slavery. Knowing that he could not effectively defend against this evidence, Gilpin declared the right of the governor not to be questioned: "Where property on board of a vessel is brought into a foreign port, the documentary evidence, whether it be a judicial decree, or the ship's papers, accompanied by possession, is the best evidence of ownership, and that to which Courts of justice invariably look." He further added, "But it is said that this evidence is insufficient, because it is in point of fact fraudulent and untrue. The ground of this assertion is, that the slaves were not property in Cuba, at the date of the document signed by the Governor General; because they had been lately introduced into that island from Africa, and persons so introduced were free. To this it is answered that, if it were so, this Court will not look beyond the authentic evidence under the official certificate of the Governor General; that, if it would, there is not such evidence as this Court can regard to be sufficient to overthrow the positive statement of that document; and that, if the evidence were even deemed sufficient to show the recent introduction of the Negroes, it does not establish that they were free at the date of the certificate."

Gilpin knew that he would get the court's attention with this argument, for if the United States felt that it could seize property from another country just because that property was on a ship within their waters, it would be tantamount to condoning piracy. The same was true if it declared papers recognized as valid by another country invalid in America. The biggest threat, of course, was that other countries could retaliate by saying the same thing about American papers. Gilpin continued, "Would this Court be justified, on evidence such as this, in setting aside the admitted certificate of the Governor General? Would such evidence, in one of our own Courts, be deemed adequate to set aside a judicial proceeding, or an act of a public functionary, done in the due exercise of his office? How, then, can it be adequate to such an end, before the tribunals of a foreign country, when they pass upon the internal municipal acts of another government; and when the endeavor is made to set them aside, in a matter relating to their own property and people?"

Of course, Gilpin knew that no matter how he might like to phrase it, there was a bigger, more morally and politically charged issue involved in the case. In fact, it was the very issue that would make the case itself one of the most famous maritime cases in history. As he stated the question, "[I]is there any difference between property in slaves and other property? They existed as property at the time of the treaty in perhaps every nation of the globe; they still exist as property in Spain and the United States; they can be demanded as property in the states of this Union to which they fly, and where by the laws they would not, if domiciled, be property. If, then, they are property, the rules laid down in regard to property extend to them. If they are found on board of a vessel, the evidence of property should be that which is recognized as the best in other cases of property ... the same rules of evidence prevailed as in other cases relative to the right of property. ... If, then, the same law exists in regard to property in slaves as in other things; and if documentary evidence, from the highest authority of the country where the property belonged, accompanied with possession, is produced; it follows that the title to the ownership of this property is as complete as is required by law."

After speaking for about two hours, Gilpin finished his argument and sat down.

Gilpin

While Adams was obviously the most well-known member of the Africans' team, he did not feel sufficiently prepared enough to argue the case when opening day rolled around, so he allowed Roger Sherman Baldwin, who had been the Africans' lawyer for longer, to take the lead.

Baldwin

After a summary of the events up until the time of the Supreme Court appeal, Baldwin began to list the reasons why the Court should indeed uphold the decisions handed down by the lower courts. In a politically astute move, he began by addressing the problem of Van Buren's interference in the case, an issue that many on both sides of the case agreed was wrong:

> "The Counsel for the Africans move the Court to dismiss this appeal, on the ground that the Executive Government of the United States had no right to become a party to the proceedings against them as property in the District Court, or to appeal from its decree.
>
> 1st. It was an unauthorized interference of the Executive with the appropriate duties of the Judiciary. ... And, it was long since remarked by an eminent jurist, that when either branch of the government usurps that part of the sovereignty which the constitution assigns to the other branch, liberty ends, and tyranny begins. The constitution designates the portion of sovereignty to be exercised by the judicial department, and among other attributes devolves upon it the cognizance of 'all cases in law or equity arising under the constitution, the laws of the United States, and treaties made or which shall be made under their authority' and 'all cases of admiralty and maritime jurisdiction and renders it sovereign, as to determinations

upon property, whenever that property is within its reach.'"

After elaborating on that argument for a while, Baldwin went on to his next point, which was that the United States had no right or obligation to protect the rights of slave ownership for people in other countries. Again, this was an excellent argument that many on both sides of the slavery issue could agree on. He explained:

> "2d. But if the Government of the United States could appear in any case as the representative of foreigners claiming property in the Court of Admiralty, it has no right to appear in their behalf to aid them in the recovery of fugitive slaves, even when domiciled in the country from which they escaped: much less the recent victims of the African slave trade, who have sought asylum in one of the free States of the Union.... The American people have never imposed it as a duty on the Government of the United States to become actors in an attempt to reduce to slavery men found in a state of freedom, by giving extra-territorial force to a foreign slave law. Such a duty would not only be repugnant to the feelings of a large portion of the citizens of the United States, but it would be wholly inconsistent with the fundamental principles of our Government, and the purposes for which it was established, as well as with its policy in prohibiting the slave trade and giving freedom to its victims."

Next, Baldwin addressed the importance of the case he was arguing. He knew that there was much more in question, and at stake, than simply the interests of those he represented. Indeed, there were many who were trying to cast the proceedings as a trial about America's "peculiar institution" – slavery – itself. The problem was that such arguments could either support or hurt Baldwin's case, and he wanted to try to make sure that it was the former rather than the latter:

> "This case is not only one of deep interest in itself as affecting the destiny of the unfortunate Africans whom I represent, but it involves considerations deeply affecting our national character in the eyes of the whole civilized world, as well as questions of power on the part of the government of the United States, which are regarded with anxiety and alarm by a large portion of our citizens. It presents, for the first time, the question whether that government, which was established for the promotion of justice, which was founded on the great principles of the Revolution, as proclaimed in the Declaration of Independence, can, consistently with the genius of our institutions, become a party to proceedings for the enslavement of human beings cast upon our shores, and found in the condition of freemen within the territorial limits of a FREE AND SOVEREIGN STATE. In the remarks I shall have occasion to make, it will be my design to appeal to no sectional prejudices, and to assume no positions in which I shall not hope to be sustained by intelligent minds from the South as well as from the North. Although I am in favor of the

broadest liberty of inquiry and discussion, — happily secured by our Constitution to every citizen, subject only to his individual responsibility to the laws for its abuse, — I have ever been of the opinion that the exercise of that liberty by citizens of one State in regard to the institutions of another should always be guided by discretion, and tempered with kindness."

After making his arguments about the rights of slaves within the United States in general, Baldwin next turned his attention to the specific question before the court, and he gave a specific and passionate answer: "We deny that Ruiz and Montes, Spanish subjects, had a right to call on any officer or Court of the United States to use the force of the government, or the process of the law for the purpose of again enslaving those who have thus escaped from foreign slavery, and sought an asylum here. We deny that the seizure of these persons by Lieutenant Gedney for such a purpose was a legal or justifiable act. How would it be -- independently of the treaty between the United States and Spain -- upon the principles of our government, of the common law, or of the law of nations? ... Is there any principle of international law, or law of comity which requires it? Are our Courts bound, and if not, are they at liberty, to give effect here to the slave trade laws of a foreign nation; to laws affecting strangers, never domiciled there, when, to give them such effect would be to violate the natural rights of men? These questions are answered in the negative by all the most approved writers on the laws of nations."

Baldwin next went on to discuss the matter of whether or not the Africans were indeed legal slaves. Rather than get bogged down in the quagmire of the honesty of the Queen of Spain, he chose to take the high ground and focus on the actions of his own country's leadership: "But it is claimed that if these Africans, though "recently imported into Cuba," were by the laws of Spain the property of Ruiz and Montes, the government of the United States is bound by the treaty to restore them; and that, therefore, the intervention of the executive in these proceedings is proper for that purpose. It has already, it is believed, been shown that even if the case were within the treaty, the intervention of the executive as a party before the judicial tribunals was unnecessary and improper, since the treaty provides for its own execution by the Courts, on the application of the parties in interest."

Responding to Gilpin's claim that the Africans were indeed merchandise, Baldwin made an effective case that anyone who had been kidnapped illegally and then fought to obtain his own freedom could not be a slave but must indeed be a free man with the same rights as any other man who was free. He was particularly interested in the fact that the slaves obtained their freedom in international waters and thus had to be free at the time they arrived in the United States:

"To render this clause of the treaty applicable to the case under consideration, it must be assumed that under the term 'merchandise' the contracting parties intended to include slaves.... ... It is believed that such a construction of the words of the treaty is not in accordance with the rules of interpretation which ought to govern our Courts; and that when there is no special reference to human beings as property, who are not acknowledged as such by the law of comity of nations generally, but only by the municipal laws of the particular nations which tolerate slavery, it cannot be presumed that the contracting parties intended to include them under the general term 'merchandise.' ... But they were not pirates.... That object was ... deliverance ... from unlawful bondage. They owed no allegiance to Spain. They were on board of the *Amistad* by constraint. Their object was to free themselves from the fetters that bound them, in order that they might return to their kindred and their home. In so doing they were guilty of no crime, for which they could be held responsible as pirates."

Of course, there was still the matter of the treaty with Spain and what Americans owed their allies, as well as anyone who might have happened upon American shores. Again, the point hinged on whether or not the Africans were free when they arrived in America, and Baldwin maintained that they were: "If, indeed, the vessel in which they sailed had been driven upon our coast by stress of weather or other unavoidable cause, and they had arrived here in the actual possession of their alleged owners, and had been slaves by the law of the country from which they sailed, and where they were domiciled, it would have been a very different question.... But in this case there has been no possession of these Africans by their claimants within our jurisdiction, of which they have been deprived, by the act of our government or its officers; and neither by the law of comity, or by force of the treaty, are the officers or Courts of the United States required, or by the principles of our government permitted to become actors in reducing them to slavery."

The next day, on February 24, John Quincy Adams rose to speak. Utilizing both the gift of speaking he inherited from his father and the classical education given to him by his mother, Quincy Adams immediately launched into an incredibly eloquent argument:

"[I]n a consideration of this case, I derive, in the distress I feel both for myself and my clients, consolation from two sources—first, that the rights of my clients to their lives and liberties have already been defended by my learned friend and colleague in so able and complete a manner as leaves me scarcely anything to say ... and secondly, ... from the thought that this Court is a Court of JUSTICE. And in saying so very trivial a thing I should not on any other occasion, perhaps, be warranted in asking the Court to consider what justice is. Justice, as defined in the Institutes of Justinian, nearly 2000 years ago, and as it felt and understood by all who understand human relations and human rights, is ... 'The constant and perpetual will to secure to everyone HIS OWN right.' And in a Court of Justice, where there are two parties present, justice demands that the rights of each party should be allowed to himself, as well as that each party has a right, to be secured and protected by the Court. This observation is important, because I appear here on the behalf of thirty-six individuals, the life and liberty of every one of whom depend on the decision of this Court."

Next, Quincy Adams addressed from his perspective the issue concerning Van Buren's interference in the case. Like Baldwin, he felt that the president was sticking his nose in where it did not belong. However, he must have been haunted somewhere in the back of his mind with similar accusations made against himself and even his beloved father in the past. While these memories did not stop him from doing his duty, it does seem to have made it particularly distasteful for him, as he mentioned: "When I say I derive consolation from the consideration that I stand before a Court of Justice, I am obliged to take this ground, because, as I shall -show, another Department of the Government of the United States has taken, with reference to this case, the ground of utter injustice, and these individuals for whom I appear, stand before this Court, awaiting their fate from its decision, under the array of the whole Executive power of this nation against them, in addition to that of a foreign nation. And here arises a consideration, the most painful of all others; in considering the duty I have to discharge, in which, in supporting the action to dismiss the appeal, I shall be obliged not only to investigate and submit to the censure of this Court, the form and manner of the proceedings of the Executive in this case, but the validity, and the motive of the reasons assigned for its interference in this unusual manner in a suit between parties for their individual rights."

Quincy Adams was only too aware that those to whom he was speaking would also be confused and perhaps even offended by his willingness to take on a fellow president. In fact, there no doubt were many who could not resist pointing out that Quincy Adams had something of an axe to grind with Van Buren since the latter had been part of the ticket that had denied him a second term in office. Not one to shy away from controversy, Quincy Adams addressed these silent concerns head on, saying, "It is, therefore, peculiarly painful to me, under present circumstances, to be under the necessity of arraigning before this Court and before the civilized world, the course of the existing Administration in this case. But I must do it. That Government is still in power, and thus, subject to the control of the Court, the lives and liberties of all my clients are in its hands. And if I should pass over the course it has pursued, those who have not kind an opportunity to examine the case and perhaps the Court itself, might decide that nothing improper had been done, and that the parties I represent had not been wronged by the course pursued by the Executive. ... The charge I make against the present Executive administration is that in all their proceedings relating to these unfortunate men, instead of that Justice, which they were bound not less than this honorable Court itself to observe, they have substituted Sympathy! —sympathy with one of the parties in this conflict of justice, and antipathy to the other. Sympathy with the white, antipathy to the black..."

In addition to the obvious racism which he knew shaped the Justices' views of the case, Quincy Adams also enumerated the wrongs that had been done to the Africans from the very beginning of their encounters with the people of America, and how such wrongs combined to create a situation in which the only real way justice could be served would be by upholding the lower courts' decisions: "The whole of my argument to show that the appeal should be dismissed, is founded on an averment that the proceedings on the part of the United States are all wrongful from the beginning. The first act, of seizing the vessel, and these men, by an officer of the navy, was a wrong. The forcible arrest of these men, or a part of them, on the soil of New York, was a wrong. After the vessel was brought into the jurisdiction of the District Court of Connecticut, the men were first seized and imprisoned under a criminal process for murder and piracy on the high seas. Then they were libeled by Lieut. Gedney, as property, and salvage claimed on them, and under that process were taken into the Custody of the marshal as property. Then they were claimed by Ruiz and Montes and again taken into custody by the court."

The longer he spoke, the more passionate Quincy Adams became about his subject. He took on the very character of the Spanish monarchy and his own Secretary of State, John Forsyth, while citing the work of popular satirist Jonathan Swift to make his point: "I know not how, in decent language, to speak of this assertion of the Secretary, that the minister of Her Catholic Majesty had claimed the Africans 'as Spanish property.' In *Gulliver's Travels*, he is represented as traveling among a nation of beings, who were very rational in many things although they were not exactly human, and they had a very cool way of using language in reference to deeds that are not laudable. When they wished to characterize a declaration as absolutely contrary to truth, they say the man has 'said the thing that is not.' It is not possible for me to express the truth respecting this averment of the Secretary of State, but by declaring that he 'has said the thing that is not.' This I shall endeavor to prove by allowing what the demand of the Spanish minister was, and that it was a totally different thing from that which was represented."

Referring to letters that passed between Forsyth (writing on behalf of the president) and members of the Court, Quincy Adams pointed out the inconsistencies of both the language and the requests. His arguments came to a grand climax when he stated, "Now, how are all these demands to be put together? First, he demands that the United States shall keep them safely, and send them to Cuba, all in a lump, the children as well as Cinqué and Grabbo. Next, he denies the power of our courts to take any cognizance of the case. And finally, that the owners of the slaves shall be indemnified for any injury they may sustain in their property. We see in the whole of this transaction, a confusion of ideas and a contradiction of positions from confounding together the two capacities in which these people are attempted to be held. One moment they are viewed as merchandise, and the next as persons. The Spanish minister, the Secretary of State, and everyone who has had anything to do with the case, all have run into these absurdities. These demands are utterly inconsistent. First, they are demanded as persons, as the subjects of Spain, to be delivered up as criminals, to be tried for their lives, and liable to be executed on the gibbet. Then they are demanded as chattels, the same as so many bags of coffee, or bales of cotton, belonging to owners, who have a right to be indemnified for any injury to their property."

Since the Spanish government's arguments were based on treaties they held with the United States, Quincy Adams next turned his attention to the pertinent portions of those treaties for the Court. Having spent most of his time thus far speaking in terms of generalities and legal principles, he turned his attention to some hypothetical but nonetheless practical applications of the principles to help the Justices see whether or not the principles could be applied in the real life setting they were facing. He also drew particular attention to the fact that the slave trade was not only illegal in the United States but was also considered piracy, a capital offence: "But the article says the same assistance shall be afforded that our own citizens would be entitled to receive in like circumstances. Let us apply the rule. Suppose the *Amistad* had been a vessel of the United States, owned and manned by citizens of the United States, and in like circumstances. Say it was a Baltimore clipper, fitted for the African slave trade, and having performed a voyage, had come back to our shores, directly or indirectly, with fifty-four African victims on board, and was thus brought into port—what would be the assistance guaranteed by our laws to American citizens, in such circumstances? The captain would be seized, tried as a pirate, and hung! And every person concerned, either as owners or on board the ship, would be severely punished. The law makes it a capital offense for the captain, and no appeal to this Court would save him from the gibbet. Is that the assistance which the Spanish minister invokes for Ruiz and Montes? That is what our laws would secure to our own citizens in like circumstances. And perhaps it would be a reward nearer their merits than the restoration of these poor Negroes to them, or enabling them to complete their voyage."

Having arrived at the heart of the matter, Quincy Adams was now ready to bring his argument home. He again addressed the issue of whether the Africans were merchandise or crew and, bringing to bear the acerbic wit that made his father famous, showed the Court just how ridiculous his opponent's arguments were: "But my clients are claimed under the treaty as merchandise, rescued from pirates and robbers. Who were the merchandise, and who were the robbers? According to the construction of the Spanish minister, the merchandise were the robbers, and the robbers were the merchandise. The merchandise was rescued out of its own hands, and the robbers were rescued out of the hands of the robbers. Is this the meaning of the treaty? Will this Court adopt a rule of construction in regard to solemn treaties that will sanction such conclusions? There is a rule in Vattel that no construction shall be allowed to a treaty which makes it absurd. Is anything more absurd than to say these forty Africans are robbers, out of whose hands they have themselves been rescued? Can a greater absurdity be imagined in construction than this, which applies the double character of robbers and of merchandise to human beings?"

Quincy Adams spent much of the rest of his time speaking out against the bad behavior of the Secretary of State as it related to the matter, but during his long first day of speaking, he could not help but notice that one among his audience appeared to be ill. Indeed, the following morning, on February 25, Justice Philip Barbour died suddenly.

Justice Barbour

The court was forced to recess in respect and did not reconvene until March 1, at which point Quincy Adams reopened his arguments against the interference of the executive branch and the unlawful influence he felt it was trying to exert on the proceedings. After a brief mention of the loss of Justice Barbour, he launched his attack:

> "I said that my confidence in a favorable result to this trial rested mainly on the ground that I was now speaking before a Court of JUSTICE. And in moving the dismissal of the appeal taken on behalf of the United States, it became my duty, and was my object to show, by an investigation of all the correspondence of the Executive in regard to the case that JUSTICE had not been the motive of its proceedings, but that they had been prompted by sympathy with one of the two parties and against the other. In support of this, I must scrutinize, with the utmost severity every part of the proceedings of the Executive Government. … I feel no unkind sentiments towards any of these gentlemen. With all of them, I am, in the private relations of life, on terms of intercourse, of the most friendly character. As to our political differences, let them pass for what they are worth, here they are nothing. … I have been of the opinion that the case of my clients was so clear, so just, so righteous, that the Executive would do well to cease its prosecution, and leave the matter as it was decided by the District Court, and allow the appeal to be dismissed. But I did not succeed, and now I cannot do justice to my clients, whose lives and liberties depend on the decision of this Court—however painful it may be, to myself or others."

Quincy Adams then proceeded to a detailed examination of the four demands made by the Secretary of State to the Court on behalf of the Spanish government. After explaining in great detail why each request was wrongfully made, or at the very least did not deserve to be heard, he concluded his arguments with a lengthy review of the case of the *Antelope*. After hearing that case in 1821, the Supreme Court returned almost 100 slaves captured off the coast of Florida to Africa. After his review of that case, Adams argued that "the opinion of the Supreme Court, as declared by the Chief Justice, in the case of the Antelope, was a fact, an authority in point, against the surrender of the *Amistad*, and in favor of the liberation of the Africans taken in her, even if they had been, when taken, in the condition of slaves."

Following his review of the *Antelope*, Quincy Adams briefly mentioned to the Court that he had not presented a case before it since 1809, more than 30 years earlier, and that he had only returned on this one occasion because of the gravity of the matter. He concluded with words that reminded the Justices of the Court's illustrious past and their obligation to its future:

> "As I cast my eyes along those seats of honor and of public trust, now occupied by you, they seek in vain for one of those honored and honorable persons whose indulgence listened then to my voice. Marshall—Cushing—Chase—Washington—Johnson—Livingston— Todd—Where are they? ... Gone! Gone! All gone! — Gone from the services which, in their day and generation, they faithfully rendered to their country. From the excellent characters which they sustained in life, so far as I have had the means of knowing, I humbly hope, and fondly trust, that they have gone to receive the rewards of blessedness on high. In taking, then, my final leave of this Bar, and of this Honorable Court, I can only ejaculate a fervent petition to Heaven, that every member of it may go to his final account with as little of earthly frailty to answer for as those illustrious dead, and that you may, every one, after the close of a long and virtuous career in this world, be received at the portals of the next with the approving sentence—'Well done, good and faithful servant; enter thou into the joy of thy Lord.'"

Gilpin rose again on March 2, 1941 to offer a rebuttal to the arguments made by Baldwin and Quincy Adams, and after he spoke for nearly three hours, the Court recessed and retired to deliberate.

John Quincy Adams in 1843

# Chapter 6: The Ruling

A page from the text of the Supreme Court decision

Justice Story

"It is also a most important consideration, in the present case, which ought not to be lost sight of, that, supposing these African negroes not to be slaves, but kidnapped, and free negroes, the treaty with Spain cannot be obligatory upon them; and the United States are bound to respect their rights as much as those of Spanish subjects." – The majority opinion of the Supreme Court in *United States v. Libellants and Claimants of the Schooner Amistad*

A week after the oral arguments ended, on March 9, Justice Joseph Story announced the Court's decision. In a 7-1 vote, the remaining Justices ruled that the Africans aboard the *Amistad* had never been the legal property of anyone:

> "[I]t is clear, in our opinion, that neither of the other essential facts and requisites has been established in proof; and the onus probandi of both lies upon the claimants

to give rise to the causes foederis. It is plain beyond controversy, if we examine the evidence, that these Negroes never were the lawful slaves of Ruiz or Montes, or of any other Spanish subjects. They are natives of Africa, and were kidnapped there, and were unlawfully transported to Cuba, in violation of the laws and treaties of Spain, and the most solemn edicts and declarations of that government. By those laws, and treaties, and edicts, the African slave trade is utterly abolished; the dealing in that trade is deemed a heinous crime; and the Negroes thereby introduced into the dominions of Spain, are declared to be free. Ruiz and Montes are proved to have made the pretended purchase of these Negroes, with a full knowledge of all the circumstances. And so cogent and irresistible is the evidence in this respect, that the District Attorney has admitted in open Court, upon the record, that these Negroes were native Africans, and recently imported into Cuba, as alleged in their answers to the libels in the case. The supposed proprietary interest of Ruiz and Montes, is completely displaced, if we are at liberty to look at the evidence of the admissions of the District Attorney."

Story further added that, in the eyes of the Court, the Africans also were guilty of no crime but instead had been "unlawfully kidnapped, and forcibly and wrongfully carried on board a certain vessel." Thus, there was no legal reason for the United States to hold them to face charges in America or return them to Spain to be tried: "If, then, these Negroes are not slaves, but are kidnapped Africans, who, by the laws of Spain itself, are entitled to their freedom, and were kidnapped and illegally carried to Cuba, and illegally detained and restrained on board of the *Amistad*; there is no pretense to say, that they are pirates or robbers. We may lament the dreadful acts, by which they asserted their liberty, and took possession of the *Amistad*, and endeavored to regain their native country; but they cannot be deemed pirates or robbers in the sense of the law of nations, or the treaty with Spain, or the laws of Spain itself; at least so far as those laws have been brought to our knowledge."

Perhaps just as importantly, the Court ruled that there was no obligation on the part of the President of the United States, or any other member of the government, to return the Africans to their homeland. Instead, they were free men and could decide for themselves where they wanted to live: "When the *Amistad* arrived she was in possession of the Negroes, asserting their freedom; and in no sense could they possibly intend to import themselves here, as slaves, or for sale as slaves. In this view of the matter, that part of the decree of the District Court is unmaintainable, and must be reversed. ... Upon the whole, our opinion is, that the decree of the Circuit Court, affirming that of the District Court, ought to be affirmed, except so far as it directs the Negroes to be delivered to the President, to be transported to Africa, in pursuance of the act of the 3d of March, 1819; and, as to this, it ought to be reversed: and that the said Negroes be declared to be free, and be dismissed from the custody of the Court, and go without delay."

Needless to say, the ruling was met with great rejoicing among the Africans and those who had so dutifully fought for their rights. As soon as they were freed from their jail cells, the abolitionists arranged for the 39 Africans who had survived the long voyage, mutiny, and imprisonment to stay in nearby Farmington, Connecticut, where they could decide what they wanted to do. While they lived in Farmington, the Africans continued to receive instruction in Christianity and the Friends Committee continued to raise money to finance a return trip to Africa for those who wished to return. Several of the abolitionists even offered to accompany the Africans to their homes and remain there as missionaries, which led to the establishment of the American Missionary Association. In turn, the American Missionary Association ultimately founded Howard University, one of the country's foremost traditionally black colleges.

In November 1841, the Africans and their missionary sponsors returned to Sierra Leone, and once there, they were reunited with their families and assisted in establishing the first of many Christian missions on the continent. However, before they left, some of the Africans wrote a letter to the one they most credited with their freedom. In May 1841, John Quincy Adams received the following, along with a most fitting gift: "We thank you very much because you make us free and because you love all Mendi people. They give you money for Mendi people and you say you will not take it, because you love Mendi people. ... Wicked people want to make us slaves but the great God who has made all things raise up friends for Mendi people he give us Mr. Adams that he may make me free and all Mendi people free. ... [W]e write this to you because you plead with the Great Court to make us free and now we are free and joyful we thank the Great God. I hope God will bless you dear friend. Mendi people will remember you when we go to our own country and we will tell all our friends about you and we will say to them Mr. Adams is a great man and he plead for us and how very glad we be and our friends will love you very much because you was a very good man and oh how joyful we shall be. ... Dear Friend I called you my Father because you set us free. Mendi people thank you very much and we will pray for you every day and night that God will keep you from danger. Dear Sir who make you to become great President over America people God – God make everything. He make men to do good and love one another. ... Mr Adams We write our names for you in this Bible that you may remember Mendi people. ... Kali, Cinqui, Cici, Kinna, Faliama, Barma, Tagino, Batu."

A memorial commemorating the *Amistad* located at Montauk Point State Park on Long Island

Battleship *Potemkin*

Unrest and Construction

At the turn of the century, the disconnect between the rulers in Moscow and the Russian population had widened to the point of producing "fatal consequences,"[1] difficult to define and impossible to predict in terms of timing, but present nonetheless. Among recent societal changes, most prominent was a belief among the working class that they could no longer survive with the current wage rates. Resentment abounded from a widespread perception of ethnic bias, and workers had no financial control over their own land. The most visible signal of political upheaval, common to many such uprisings, was the radicalization of higher education.

Through the first years of the new century, a majority of the public maintained its blind faith in the tsarist system, but that view changed in January of 1905, when the 200,000 workers marched in St. Petersburg on a day that came to be known as Bloody Sunday. The march had been intended as a peaceful demonstration, conducted with the hope that the tsar would hear their plight. Its trappings were banners and icons in lieu of guns. Nicholas was still affectionately

---

[1] Bright Hub Engineering, Russian Battleship Potemkin – www.brighthubengineering.com/marine-history/124041-russian-battleship-potemkin/

addressed "little father,"[2] and the people felt confident he would surely sympathize. Instead of the audience they craved, the crowd was fired upon by Nicholas's troops, killing over 1,000, although alternate accounts set the number at much less. Father Gapon, spokesman for the demonstration, was heard to cry out, "There is no God anymore. There is no tsar."[3]

    Despite their appeal to Tsar Nicholas II for improved working conditions and the establishment of a popular assembly, troops indiscriminately opened fire, killing over 1,000. In addition to the mass shooting, many more were "ridden down"[4] on a day that would come to be known as Bloody Sunday. In the coming months, thousands of such uprisings were met with the same response.

Tsar Nicholas II and his family

    Reaction to the slaughter spread quickly, and by February revolts had spread all the way to the

---

[2] History Today, Bloody Sunday in St. Petersburg, January 1, 2005 – www.history.com/richard-Cavendish/bloody-sunday-st-petersburg
[3] History Today, Bloody Sunday
[4] The Romanov Family

Caucus region in the south. On February 4, the Grand Duke Sergei Alexandrovich was killed in an orchestrated assassination; as he rode in his carriage through Moscow, the assailant strode forward seemingly out of nowhere and dropped a nitroglycerin bomb in his victim's lap. The Grand Duke, blamed in part for the Khodynka Tragedy, was already a vulnerable target.

Grand Duke Sergei Alexandrovich

The carriage after the assassination

By February 6, uprisings had erupted in the region of Kursk, yet Nicholas did not respond to any of these until February 8, when he ordered the creation of an assembly charged with advising on constitutionally-based reforms. The rejection of this gesture only lent impetus to the uprisings. By March, the strikes had reached the Urals and Siberia, and in May, the end of the Russo-Japanese War was signaled when the Baltic Fleet was sunk by an enemy once thought to be easily overcome. The ships took seven months sailing around to Japan only to meet a quick and inglorious end at the hands of superior enemy forces. The previous year, Russia was forced to surrender Port Arthur to the Japanese, and morale among naval forces still in Russian harbors plummeted.

In June of 1905, soldiers were used to put down strikes in Lodz, and by June 18, uprisings in Odessa had been ruthlessly halted with a level of brutality seared into the long-term Russian memory. On June 14 and over the following 10 days, a mutiny took place aboard the battleship Potemkin as another enduring symbol of unrest. Nicholas's love of photography as a promotional tool backfired, as parts of the Potemkin rebellion were caught on film.

On August 1, he put forward the First Conference of the Peasants' Union in an attempt to stem the fury. Five days later, he delivered a manifesto calling for the creation of a Duma, which was also rejected as insufficient and inauthentic. The war with Japan ended by August 23, leaving Russia's naval force, already aware of the Potemkin mutiny, even more disgruntled by the decimation of the fleet at the Battle of Tsushima.

In the month of September, a printers' strike hit Moscow, and by October, it had burgeoned into a full strike. In December, the St. Petersburg Soviet was arrested en masse. As distant protests lost steam, the failure of the Moscow rioters to complete their coup barely saved Nicholas in the end. Soon after, the Tsar and his son Alexei were given honorary membership in the Union of the Russian People, a gesture that was readily accepted by the shaken monarch. Parties such as the Marxist Russian Social Democratic Labor Party and the Socialist Revolutionary Party, organizations once unthinkable, flourished in tandem with the Union of Zemstvo Constitutionalists and Union of Liberation, established within the previous two years.

Despite Nicholas's concessions on freedom of speech, the right of citizens to choose their own religion, personal immunity, and other "basics of civil liberties,"[5] the workers' right to national representation was entirely absent in his manifesto. It is probable that the masses did not fully understand the significance of the new Duma, by which no law could be enacted without the body's agreement, even by the royal family.

In time, the memory of the troubles in 1905 gradually faded. Nicholas fell back into his former autocratic habits wherever he could, strengthening the Franco-Russian alliance and in general pursuing a policy of "European pacification"[6] after the major wars of the 19th century. At the same time, the relationship between the palace and the Duma grew continuously worse.

Design and construction of warships such as the *Potemkin* began in the final two decades of the 19th century in an attempt to replace the "ironclads" of the previous naval era. The new vessels came to be classified under the category of "pre-dreadnought," predating more advanced propulsion systems, armaments, and fuel sources. With a length of almost 130 yards, *Potemkin* was to be manned by a complement of up to 800 men, making for tight quarters.

By 1895, plans for the ship's construction were well under way, and crews began work in December of 1897. *Potemkin*'s structure was "laid down" at the Nikolayev Admiralty Shipyard on October 19, 1898. Two years later, on October 9, 1900, she was launched. Her first outing was a transfer to the Crimean port of Sevastopol for fitting out on July 4, 1902. Commissioned in 1903 and nearly complete, *Potemkin* was to be the pride of the new Black Sea Naval Forces. In that year, she began the customary sea trials, which continued until the gun turrets had been completed, nearly two years later. The new battleship was christened by its full name, *Kniaz Potemkin Tavrichevsky,* a title conferred in honor of the Russian soldier and statesman Prince Grigory Potemkin, who was largely responsible for building the original Black Sea Fleet under

---

[5] Russiapedia
[6] Russiapedia

Catherine the Great. The *Potemkin* was intended to serve as a counterpart to the best of rival navies, and others of its type were to follow.

Potemkin

An early 20th century picture of the shipyard

Potemkin's overall length at the waterline came to about 371.5 feet with a deck length of 378 feet. Her beam width was 73 feet and her draft 27 feet. This made her unsuitable for shallow port water, but that was not her intended mission. The ship was propelled by two three-cylinder engines, totaling 10,000 horsepower, and with 22 boilers in simultaneous operation, each engine drove one propeller. Eight boilers in the forward boiler room were oil-fired, in contrast to the general use of coal as a fuel, but in January of 1904, Potemkin experienced a serious oil leak, resulting in a devastating fire, so the navy converted all of her boilers to coal-firing units, at a cost of over 20,000 rubles. Fully loaded, she carried approximately 1,100 tons of coal.

The ship at anchor in the 1900s

The projected range of travel without restocking was calculated at 3,000 nautical miles, roughly equivalent to 3,700 land miles, based upon a speed of 10 knots, or 12 miles per hour. Thus, the navy was elated to find that on October 31, 1903, *Potemkin* reached a speed of 16.5 knots, or 19 mph.

The original designs called for outfitting *Potemkin* with long-range guns, but that plan was vetoed by General Admiral Grand Duke Alexei Alexandrovich, who believed that such armaments were inappropriate for the confines of the Black Sea. For short range weaponry, the ship was fit with four 40 caliber, 305 mm guns mounted in twin turrets, both fore and aft. These were electronically operated, but the rate of fire was exceedingly slow, discharging only one round every four minutes. Despite the absence of open-sea range, *Potemkin* could fire with adequate accuracy at a distance of 13,000 yards, or 12,000 meters, and carried 60 rounds of ammunition for each gun, sufficient for protracted battles. Her armor at the waterline measured nine inches in thickness.

General Admiral Grand Duke Alexei Alexandrovich

Accompanying the updated technology of the Russian Navy was a time-worn command structure and obsolete approach to discipline that preserved the "harsh conditions and brutal punishments of an earlier age."[7] Rights of non-enlisted men were scarcely more enlightened than they had been several centuries prior, and the ship's personnel did not boast the most seasoned officers or crewmen. The experience level was negligible, as battle-tested veterans had been sent to the Pacific to face the Japanese in the Russo-Japanese War, a confrontation that reached its climax in May of 1905 at the Battle of the Tsushima Strait. That effort took most of the experienced officers and enlisted men from the Baltics and Black Sea, leaving *Potemkin* with raw recruits, officers that have been described as "the dregs of the nobility,"[8] and utterly without concern for the personal well-being of their crews.

---

[7] Richard Cavendish, The Mutiny on the Potemkin, History Today – www.historytoday.com/richard-cavendish/mutiny-potemkin
[8] Neil Bascomb, *Red Mutiny, Eleven Fateful Days on the Battleship Potemkin*, May 27, 2007, Houghton Mifflin

In addition to the tsar's habit of overcompensating, and in many cases simply assessing a situation incorrectly, Nicholas had a miserably poor record of success in a variety of military engagements. Of course, this woeful state of military affairs would continue into World War I and contribute to his eventual downfall, but over a decade earlier, the Japanese fleet was considered to represent an easy Russian victory in 1904 and should have buoyed Russian spirits, or so Nicholas thought.

Japan's naval forces attacked Port Arthur, a Russian naval base in China. The Baltic fleet was sent, under Admiral Zinovy Petrovich Rozhestvensky, to join the Pacific fleet in order to overwhelm the Japanese contingent. But the Tsar's "easy victory" was not to be, despite having the best of Russia's naval leadership present in the theater. The arriving fleet demonstrated its incompetence from the outset by mistakenly attacking a group of British trawlers, sinking four of them and almost igniting an war between the two countries, but even once they engaged the correct enemy, the captains proved grossly unprepared, and the ships too unwieldy and slow.

In hindsight, the Battle of Tsushima is generally considered among the most "under-funded, ill-equipped and poorly led"[9] ventures in Russian naval history. Having only come out of isolation to the wider world a few decades before, Japan not only "tore the Russian fleet apart"[10] under the leadership of Admiral Heihachiro Togo, it did much the same to Rozhestvestky's second fleet, arriving from the Baltics in support. Of the 45 Russian warships gathered at Tsushima after months of sailing, only 10 were able to escape to safety. Four reached Vladivostok with considerable difficulty, while the remaining six found protection in neutral ports. Japan became the first Asian power to defeat the forces of a major European state, forcing Russia to abandon its expansionist policies to the east as Port Arthur fell, despite skirmishes continuing through May. With that, Nicholas surrendered his dream of dominance over Korea and Manchuria, a blow to Russia's customary bent toward expansionism.

An added blow was the major defeat of Russian land forces in March of 1904. Coupled with the St. Petersburg catastrophe, rebellion seemed inevitable, and it was more likely to erupt in the navy than anywhere else. Far greater than physical damage done to the Russian fleet was the blow to Russian morale among the citizenry and members of the military, both of which were severely "demoralized"[11] and in need of someone to blame. The international humiliation was soothed, in part, by a face-saving treaty brokered by President Theodore Roosevelt of the United States, and some of the criticism reserved for Nicholas's government was heaped, instead, on military officers.

The Mutiny

Battleships have always been, to some degree, symbolic of the state that deploys them. Russia

---

[9] Neil Bascomb
[10] Bright Hub Engineering
[11] Bright Hub Engineering

began with relatively few considering the geographical demands, and what remained was paltry following the embarrassment at the hands of Japan. The emasculation of the fleet that spurred resentment against the officer class intensified their reflex to clamp down even harder on crewmen, whose belief in the command structure had already been compromised. Faced with an environment "notorious for poor conditions"[12] and the continuation of increasingly "horrific disciplinary measures,"[13] relations aboard the *Potemkin* teetered delicately upon any errant moment that might spark the breakdown of order. That moment arrived unexpectedly, when an onboard conflict ensued over the quality of the crew's food.

At the turn of the 20th century, Russia was in transition between two calendars. According to the former measurement, the mutiny aboard the *Potemkin* took place on June 14, 1905. Others cite the date as June 27. The *Potemkin* was not involved, and never would be, in any battle, and it was in no immediate danger from any external threat. She had been sent to Tender Island off the Ukrainian coast for routine training exercises, including "gun tests" and "target firing."[14] Officers suspected nothing amiss and failed to take into sufficient account that they had among the crew one of the most ferocious advocates for revolution in the entire Russian military, the fiery torpedo quartermaster Afanasy Matyushenko, who would be largely responsible for the outward expressions of the *Potemkin*'s 1905 rebellion.

---

[12] Bright Hub Engineering
[13] Bright Hub Engineering
[14] Marxist.com

Matyushenko (in the white shirt left of center)

Matyushenko was the son of a peasant family in the Kharkiv region of Ukraine in the village of Dergachi. He had already been accused of bringing foreign ideologies that he had learned in his big city travels home to his village by his late teens. As a result, he was forced to flee his home before the age of 18. Serving as a railway machinist in addition to other temporary jobs, Matyushenko was drafted into the Russian Imperial Navy in 1900 at the age of 21. A member of the secretive Social Democratic Party, he was notorious for spreading anti-tsarist sentiments and fanning anti-government passions throughout the *Potemkin*'s crew, after having already establishing several successful "revolutionary cells"[15] elsewhere. He walked a fine line at all times, since political parties of any sort were illegal in Russia. Still, he continued to emerge as a prominent dissident, even after being selected by the *Potemkin*'s crew as head of the Ship's Commission.

Due in part to Matyushenko's covert agitation against the ship's officers, *Potemkin* was already far from a "happy ship,"[16] and the crew was rife with "revolutionary sympathies,"[17] more than

---
[15] Libcom.org, Matiushenko, Afanasy Nikolaevich, 1879-1907 – www.libcom.org/history/matiushenko-afansy-nikolaevich-1877-1907
[16] Richard Cavendish

her fellow ships in the fleet. The impending revolt aboard the *Potemkin* was not intended to be "entirely spontaneous,"[18] as Matyushenko had scheduled it months before, in league with fellow sailor Grigory Valenchuk, for it to commence in the month of August.

The planned revolt had not been the first one among Russian warships, nor had it been the first sign of unrest within Russian ports. Actions had already taken place in Sevastopol, Vladivostok on the Pacific, and in Kronstadt. However, the mutiny originating on board the *Potemkin* had been intended as a coordinated action between all ports and fleets, based on the belief that the sense of indignation rampant in other segments of the population would catch fire, creating a domino effect. Matyushenko and Valenchuk labored for nearly half a year to gain support among the crew, "arranging, preaching, cajoling, [and] teaching the art of resistance."[19] A sizeable nucleus of disgruntled mutineers under Matyushenko's influence had already outlined the action they believed would result in a fleet-wide insurrection. The "concerted blow"[20] struck against the officer class and extended aristocracy would lead the way to enlisting the peasant class in widespread revolt, powerful enough to sweep Nicholas II from the throne. With the strikes occurring on land and a deepening gravity of the naval losses in Japan fueling the "impending revolutionary storm,"[21] Matyushenko held to August as the ideal time to ignite the mutiny. However, the unexpected incident aboard the *Potemkin* had triggered the plan prematurely before the revolutionary fervor across Russia had the necessary time in which to congeal into unified resistance. Matyushenko was unable to restrain himself from abandoning the August timetable, and inaccurately viewed an isolated, onboard insult leveled by officers at the crew as a more potent omen than it eventually proved to be.

June 14, 1905, according to the old calendar, was described in eyewitness accounts as a "muggy"[22] summer's day. Tempers were already short when the cooks complained about the supply of meat taken aboard to be used in the crew's borscht. It was, in their words, "riddled with maggots,"[23] and therefore inedible. A ship's doctor was summoned to examine the meat in question, and decided that the "maggots" were only flies' eggs. His conclusion was that the meat was of excellent quality, and that it would be safe to eat it after washing it with water. According to author Neal Bascomb, who chronicled the 11-day incident, "order suddenly disintegrated, [and] life and death decisions were made in seconds."[24]

Matyushenko's account, although understandably partisan in every case, is rich in detail as the memoir of a central participant in the revolt. In his view, the isolation of the *Potemkin* in the

---

[17] Richard Cavendish
[18] Bright Hub Engineering
[19] Neal Bascomb
[20] Evan Andrews, The Mutiny on the Battleship Potemkin, History.com – www.history.com/news/mutiny-on-the-battleship-potemkin-110-years-ago
[21] Marxist.com
[22] Neal Bascomb
[23] Evan Andrews
[24] Neal Bascomb

Tender Island region was a contributor to the premature ignition of the conflict. Arriving at the island, the *Potemkin*'s accompanying supply vessel, *Torpedo Boat 67*, continued on to Odessa to procure provisions, returning in the evening of the same day. The slab of meat that was to fortify the crew's soup had been hung by hooks on the spar deck, and the presence of maggots was not discovered until the following morning. It was Matyushenko who had openly suggested an inspection, being quoted as saying, "Show it to the doctor, then have it thrown overboard."[25]

Captain Evgeny Golikov, known on board as "the dragon,"[26] was already unpopular after suspending the crew's bathing privileges, but he complied. The Honorable Counsellor Smirnov was summoned to the spar deck. In Matyushenko's recollection, Smirnov drew close to the hanging meat, put his pince-nez on, and sniffed before declaring the meat to be of perfectly good quality. Remarking that the crew was being "merely faddy"[27] in its refusal, he conceded that the meat should be washed with water to further appease any hesitation. Golikov responded by posting a sentry to guard the meat around the clock. The lone guard was supplied with pencil and paper, and instructed to take down the names of anyone who approached. The order successfully prevented any tampering with the meat, as no one from the crew came near, but Matyushenko also recalled that the crew had been preoccupied and offended by the superior treatment offered to Japanese prisoners.

---

[25] Marxist.com
[26] Neal Bascomb
[27] Marxist.com

Captain Golikov

At the sounding of the dinner bell, Golikov lined up the entire crew on deck, and issued the command, "Whoever wants to eat the borsht, step forward."[28] Ippolit Gilyarovsky, *Potemkin*'s second-in-command, kept his hand near his revolver throughout the confrontation, and upon the captain's command, threatened to shoot anyone who did not comply. Many among the crew lost their nerve and stepped forward, most of them men with long terms of service, "bosuns, [and] some of the officers."[29] The hard-liners behind Matyushenko, however, stood their ground, and a few broke ranks to hide behind a gun turret.

A company of Marine Guards was summoned as another group of crewmen attempted to bolt, but were halted. A tarpaulin was ordered thrown over the mutineers, through which they would be shot so that a minimal amount of blood would stain the deck. Matyushenko claimed to have exhorted his colleagues with the pronouncement, "Enough of Golikov drinking our blood. Grab rifles and ammunition…take over the ship!"[30] At that point, Matyushenko and Valenchuk ran to

---

[28] Evan Andrews
[29] Marxist.com
[30] Evan Andrews

the weapons room and armed themselves, encountering a vicious firefight in their attempt to return to the deck. Allies of the two sailors spread across the ship as the Marine Guards prepared to fire, but they hesitated at Matyushenko's continued bellowing, "Comrades, don't forget your oath. Don't shoot at your own men."[31] Captain Golikov responded by drawing a gun on Matyushenko and ordering him to drop his weapon, but the sailor replied, "Get off the ship. This is the peoples' ship, and not yours."[32] The gun muzzles of the Marine Guards dropped toward the deck, and the officers were left alone to face a crew with an advantage in numbers of 30 to 1.

The numerous eyewitness and secondary accounts of the altercation between officers and crew are at odds regarding the timing at which the sailors' delegation attempted to speak calmly with the highest-ranking officers. It is known the party was headed by Valenchuk, and it is suggested Matyushenko's co-revolutionary expressed himself "so plainly"[33] that the second-in-command, Gilyarovsky, pulled a revolver and shot him dead on the spot. The vastly outnumbered officers were, in most cases, rounded up and put under heavy guard. Gilyarovsky was seized by the crew and thrown overboard, only to be shot and killed by Matyushenko, who fired from a gun turret above while Gilyarovsky was floundering in the water. The captain was discovered hiding in one of the staterooms with Chief Artillery Officer Neopkoev. Golikov threw himself at Matyushenko's feet, but Matyushenko replied that his fate lay in the hands of the crew. Both officers were immediately shot. The ship's surgeon was also killed and several officers were "shut away in a cabin,"[34] except for one Lieutenant Ton, who had amassed a particularly horrific reputation for his treatment of the crew. Ton pleaded for a personal audience with Matyushenko, who agreed to meet on deck. Once the two were close, Ton pulled his revolver and fired, missing his target and wounding a sailor standing nearby. He was immediately shot to death by the others.

---

[31] Marxist.com
[32] Marxist.com
[33] Richard Cavendish
[34] Richard Cavendish

Gilyarovsky

 A small band of remaining officers managed to reach the escort vessel *Ismail*, a small torpedo boat. They raised anchor and attempted to steam to Odessa for protection, but shots fired from the *Potemkin*'s 47 mm and 75 mm guns forced them to abort the escape. They were taken back aboard and locked in a cabin. A dozen were arrested and informed their fate would be determined later. Several more officers, the large ship's portrait of Nicholas II, and the offending meat, were all "chucked"[35] overboard together. Within 30 frantic minutes, the mutiny aboard *Potemkin* was complete, and the crew's fate relied entirely on larger Russia's willingness to enter into a state of revolution with her. Any other outcome would be dire for the *Potemkin*, trapped within the confines of the Black Sea and with no clear path to the open ocean.

Odessa

 Matyushenko was selected as chairman of a new "People's Committee,"[36] numbering up to 25 sailors by some accounts, although those close to the event place the committee personnel at around a dozen. With almost all of the officers under guard–except for those crucial to specific ship operations–the *Potemkin* hoisted the red flag, more as a signal of revolution than the insignia of any specific anti-tsarist faction. Cheered by the outcome of the incident, Matyushenko insisted on moving forward with the plan, urging the crew on with shouts of "The great day is near,"[37] despite the overthrow of the previously planned timetable. In an

---

[35] Bright Hub Engineering
[36] Richard Cavendish
[37] Evan Andrews

unexpectedly impromptu rebellion, *Potemkin* and her crew of non-commissioned sailors began a sea journey of 11 days, "prowling"[38] around the Black Sea in an attempt to restock its coal and food supplies, and to ignite a collaborative revolution wherever it could find a willing consensus.

The nearest and most promising destination was the southernmost port city of Odessa, already experiencing widespread unrest at the hands of multiple, albeit fragmented, factions. As she got under way, *Potemkin*'s radio message read, "The crimes of the autocratic government have exhausted all patience."[39] Designed primarily for Odessa, Matyushenko's diatribe continued, declaring "the government wants to drown the country in blood,"[40] and that it had forgotten that troops on shore and at sea were all "sons of the oppressed people."[41]

To the crew of the *Potemkin*, it must have seemed as if Odessa was nearly a foregone conclusion, such was the state of social chaos there. Buildings around the harbor were burning, and sporadic strikes had broken out over the previous two weeks, growing to citywide proportions, Clashes between the police, Cossacks, and demonstrators from various factions were commonplace. The trains and trams had ground to a standstill, and most small merchants had closed their shops. Most of Odessa's industry had been contained within numerous small plants, making full cooperation for general strikes more difficult to achieve. The phenomenon of a government battleship arriving in Odessa harbor, manned by a rebellious crew of non-officers, was impossible to ignore. By the time *Potemkin* appeared on June 15, large crowds had gathered at the waterfront to greet her, unsure of what might occur next, but intoxicated by the story. In order to make the strongest possible statement, the small party that rowed ashore brought with them the body of Grigory Valenchuk. He was placed upon a bier where the public could see him on the Richelieu Steps, the main entrance to the city from the sea and site of the famous scene depicting the slaughter of private citizens in Eisenstein's famous film, two decades later. The statue of Richelieu stands at the top, paying tribute to the city's first mayor. The note pinned to Valenchuk's chest read, "This is the body of Valenchuk, killed by the Commander for having told the truth."[42] To emphasize the success of their venture, the note added, "Retribution has been meted out to the Commander."[43]

As the day wore on, numbers within the crowd swelled. Thousands arrived, many bringing flowers to Valenchuk's bier and food for the crew. The landing of the shore party was well-calculated, and had several missions in its lengthy agenda. The first was to procure provisions through either purchase or gift, and to restock the coal supplies. Politically, the act of bringing Valenchuk's body ashore with the crew's manifesto was intended to make clear to the population the seeds of revolution had been planted, and that *Potemkin* awaited only a collective response.

---

[38] Evan Andrews
[39] Russapedia, On This Day: Russia in a Click, 27 June – www.russapedia.com/on-this-day/june-27/
[40] Russapedia
[41] Russapedia
[42] Richard Cavendish
[43] Richard Cavendish

The shore party offered a detailed account of what had taken place at Tender Island, so that news of government aggression would be known throughout the city as recounted by the crew. Of equal importance was to draw up a plea for unity, not only with the population, but with the Cossacks and gendarmes, including the commanding French colonel. The *Potemkin* crew needed to rid itself of the burdensome remaining officers who refused to convert to the revolutionary cause by leaving them ashore. This was, for them, the best outcome if they were able to elude the angered mob. A handful of the original officers remained on board, including the engineer Kovalenko. Alexeyev, a mid-shipman, had been set free, but returned to the ship as a captain with limits placed on his authority, "under observation of the crew."[44] Lieutenant Kaluzhny and Dr. Galenko were both set free.

The *Potemkin* shortly after the mutiny

A.P. Brzhezovsky, at first an anonymous face among the participants in the *Potemkin* rebellion, author of *Eleven Days on the Potemkin*, described the scene in Odessa as being in a state of pandemonium. The increasingly drunken crowd, he observes, made movement through the streets by the harbor all but impossible, and in time, the docks were set afire. Everyone wanted to get a look at Valenchuk, and the citizenry displayed an overtly emotional response to his death, as the crew had hoped they would. According to Brzhezovsky, a nearby orator spoke to all the groups who came to witness the scene, with chants of "Death to the tyrants"[45] resounding through the streets. In a fit of passion, he rushed to the speaker's platform and called upon all sailors aboard the *Potemkin* to come ashore and join him in a march through the center of town in order to further inspire the resistance. The crowd moved as one, but hundreds of whistles

---
[44] Marxist.com
[45] Marxist.com

sounded simultaneously as a company of Cossacks entered the area to confront the crowd. Between pleas to the Cossacks to put their weapons away, and threats to turn Odessa into a "heap of ruins,"[46] the commander of the port lost confidence in the Cossacks as a sole deterrent, as they were largely native to that region and formerly part of the Ottoman Empire. To preserve objectivity on the part of government soldiers, extra regiments were called in from greater distances as reinforcements. However, when these troops attempted to seize Valenchuk's body, and in doing so remove the object of the crowd's emotion, the ship's shore party intervened. Between *Potemkin* crewmembers and an indignant crowd, the troops were turned back, leading to a declaration of martial law throughout the city.

Matyushenko's highest priority was to establish a unified sense of purpose among the factions of the Social Democratic Party. The illegal party had been formed in the city of Minsk over seven years prior. The ship's committee issued a call for representatives of all anti-tsarist organizations, as they were able, to meet aboard the *Potemkin*. Not only were these organizations poorly coordinated with one another, but in most cases, they lived in a state of overt hostility toward any approach to revolution other than their own. Some representatives did meet with the crew in order to inform them of events taking place in the town, but some of the *Potemkin*'s sailors added to the problem by rejecting the notion of entertaining strangers on the ship.

For some, the idea of expanding the revolution beyond the *Potemkin* meant the surrender of autonomy as members of the original uprising. The meetings were brief and woefully unsuccessful in uniting the Bolsheviks and Mensheviks in particular. The former favored an armed insurrection in every case, while the latter sought a peaceful path forward. The Bolsheviks were in the minority, but always acted with the most public aggression. To that end, Vladimir Lenin favored the engaging of "disciplined professional revolutionaries"[47] for a successful coup in lieu of easily disheartened peasant groups, and yet favored the worker and peasant classes for positions of leadership. The outward passion of the Bolsheviks eventually won out, and they played a driving role in the 1905 uprising with "liberal rhetoric…strikes…student riots, and terrorist assassinations."[48] Ironically, the larger organization of Mensheviks who were politically trampled by Lenin's faction, translated their party name to "those in the minority."[49] The Bolshevik view that the country should be led by workers and serfs, such as those serving on the *Potemkin* crew, was unthinkable and "utopian."[50] For the Bund, representing Jewish interests, the process was even more urgent, as anti-Semitic actions had become overt government policy. Their plan, submitted to the ship, required the mutineers to land a strong party onshore, and to march at the head of a massive demonstration through the main square. The march was to culminate with Valenchuk's public burial, in an outright invitation to a confrontation with troops

---

[46] Marxist.com
[47] Encyclopaedia Britannica
[48] Encyclopaedia Britannica
[49] Encyclopaedia Britannica
[50] C.N Trueman, History Learning Site, UK – The 1905 Russian Revolution – www.historylearningsite.co.uk/modern-world-history-1918-to-1980/russia-1900-to-1939/the-1905-russian-revolution

and police. At the first signs of conflict, sailors at the head of the march would call on them to put their weapons down, join them in freeing the city from the tsarist government, and fraternize in the search for a solution, unifying the town's factions.

Lenin

The ultimate aim of such a plan was to diffuse and render "all the resources"[51] within reach of the government useless. In the event of the demonstration's failure, the *Potemkin* was to bombard the city, aiming its large guns at government installations as precisely as possible. In the end, however, the plan had been deemed inadvisable by the *Potemkin* crew, many of whom were opposed to an armed assault on the town which might risk killing supporters of the revolt. The People's Committee feared that if the crew became geographically split, not enough crew representation would be present either to lead the march or operate the ship. In addition, the Mensheviks were dragging their feet on the issue of confrontation.

---

[51] Marxist.com

Matyushenko expressed utter scorn for their bent toward diplomacy, and wanted to bomb the city indiscriminately to raise popularity for widespread rebellion. The crew, however, hesitated after firing only two shots from six-inch guns, both of which missed the Odessa Town Theater, where the Military Council had been meeting. More than one account claimed it was a spy on board who had altered the aim of the guns, and such inefficiency made for one of the only instances in which Matyushenko had been deterred. Such was the difficulty of what was to become the "abortive revolution"[52] of 1905. Had the revolution been ignited two months later, as previously planned, it is doubtful anti-tsarist factions would have made sufficient progress toward a consensus for a successful outcome. Added to that, a good deal more than party unity among the resistance was required. A fully committed revolution depended on the emotional preparedness of large cross-sections of the population, including a "tenuous alliance between liberal society and a growing workers' movement"[53] that constantly ebbed and flowed. Subsets of liberal constituencies, including "educated society, urban labor, nationalities, and the peasantry,"[54] were as ill-configured for forward motion as political factions were in "disarray."[55]

The liberal movement in the form of local governments had been comprised of a "loose collection"[56] of gentry Zemstvo, a widespread form of local liberal government. Generally included were "teachers, doctors and lawyers, agronomists, engineers, and statisticians."[57] Their place in history has often been as the vanguard of one revolution, and the first to be executed when the counter-revolution arrived. Bolsheviks, representing the most poorly organized resistance party of all, were nevertheless vociferous in attempting to pull the people toward armed rebellion. Ideologically blinded, they could not reach a state of compromise with any other movement, regardless of the stakes.

On the other side, the national government had been equally fragmented due, in large part, to a "lethally indecisive"[58] Nicholas II, so that the idea of impending revolution hung in a limbo from which no party could obtain a "quick, decisive victory."[59] Throughout 1905, resistance against the tsar remained "provisional,"[60] regardless of the underlying emotion, and as history later revealed, would not muster the necessary synchronicity for another decade or more. On all sides, disagreements over methods preventing a unified resistance remained as only one part of the anti-tsarists' problem. In addition, every group either had its own agenda, or lacked one entirely, other than the impetus to overthrow the system. The Kadets, members of the Constitutional Party, or the Party of the People's Freedom, had only been founded a few months prior by the

---

[52] Richard Cavendish
[53] Abraham Archer, The Revolution of 1905: Russia in Disarray, Review by Scott J. Seregny, The Russian Review, Vol. 48 No. 2 (April 1989) p 184
[54] Abraham Archer
[55] Abraham Archer
[56] History.com
[57] History.com
[58] Raymond A. Esthers, Nicholas II and the Russo-Japanese War, *The Russian Review* Vol. 40 No. 4 (Oct. 1981) p396
[59] Abraham Archer
[60] Abraham Archer

Union of Liberation, and had yet to express few other desires past the creation of an effective constitution. The peasants' wish list emphasized more acquisition of land and an increased authority with which to control it. The Nationalists created no blueprint for life past the tsar's overthrow, and were ambivalent toward almost any replacement system put forth. They were, however, adamant about secession from Russia. The phantom constitution of 1905 pleased the Kadets and the middle class, but did not directly address other groups. Peasants of the era had developed "little political consciousness,"[61] and no distinct individual stepped forward to offer leadership for dissident political organizations. The one galvanizing figure speaking for the Bolsheviks, Vladimir Lenin, was still in exile. Contrary to long-term Bolshevik goals, the Nationalists had no great desire for "political or social radicalism," besides wanting out of the Russian contract. The Social Democratic Labor Party did its best to support the *Potemkin* uprising, but M.I. Vasil'ev-luzhin, the representative sent by Lenin from exile, was not able to reach the region in time to capitalize on the unrest or meet with the central players. Even among the crew of the *Potemkin*, the thirst for outright rebellion was not likely unanimous, and felt in varying degrees. Later accounts suggest that not all of the sailors desired to serve as the "vanguard of an upcoming revolution,"[62] and despite being dragged along in fear of what might befall them if they resisted, remained unconvinced of Matyushenko's "illusory plan."[63]

On June 15, the *Potemkin* crew captured a smaller vessel named the *Vekka*, bound from Nikolayev, home to the *Potemkin*'s original shipyard, to Odessa. The mutineers arrested both the captain and the full complement of officers, put them on shore unarmed, and converted the *Vekka* into a medical ship. The *Vekka* crew willingly joined the *Potemkin*, shoring up losses and offering a good sign for later success in winning over the remainder of the navy. On the same day, two delegations arrived from two full regiments, the *Ismail* and the *Danube*. Anxious to know the *Potemkin*'s intent, they expressed a willingness to join the crew in their revolt if the rogue ship were to take decisive action, such as participation in the much-debated march. They further promised that if the *Potemkin* fired on the city, their regiments would withhold return fire. Matyushenko's wish to attack the town aside, the general hesitation aboard the *Potemkin* held, and the crew's new alliance with the regiments ashore went untested. In one instance, a force of police and gendarmes attempted to board the ship, but were forced to retreat, throwing their swords into the water as they went. Some historians of the Russian Empire's final years suggest that the *Potemkin*'s arrival in the port of Odessa served as a convenient camouflage for human abuses regularly conducted by the government. Cossacks, police, and troops, through the height of the civilian uprising, were given permission to overact in a number of atrocities directed against political dissidents and Jewish enclaves.

Potemkin could not remain within the port of Odessa in a state of indecision, because news of the mutiny reached the tsar in short order, and he instructed navy vessels and troops to quash it in

---

[61] Slideplayer
[62] Neal Bascomb
[63] Stefan-Catalin Trofin

no uncertain terms. Fearing a contagion of revolt, either on land or on other ships, his orders conveyed an urgency that "each hour of delay may cost rivers of blood in the future."[64] Within hours, two squadrons steamed toward Odessa with the intent to either force *Potemkin*'s surrender, or to sink her.

While the crew waited for the tsar's ships, the situation in Odessa eroded as troops took up positions around the crowd that had gathered in the evening. Riots had broken out during the afternoon, and numerous buildings were burning. Whether a specific action caused soldiers to open fire on civilians is uncertain, but the order to do so brought repeated volleys sent into the densely-packed crowd as the *Potemkin* sat silently by, afraid to fire on a sympathetic crowd. Cossacks cut a "bloody swath"[65] through the throng with sabers, leaving over 2,000 killed, and more than 1,000 seriously wounded. Once short-term calm had been restored, Valenchuk's burial was permitted, although the *Potemkin* crew's plea for general amnesty was rejected. Despite the "skillful agitation"[66] and the "bungling"[67] of many officers, the demonstrators lost the momentum necessary to overthrow the city. The government conveniently laid the blame for Odessa's unrest at the feet of the city's Jews, who were to undergo a series of vicious pogroms in the following three months. At that time, hundreds would be killed and enormous bodies of property would be confiscated.

Many of the news reports received in the West on the ongoing drama came through Britain, who had as many as 15 ships in the port of Odessa when the *Potemkin* arrived. At the turn of the 20th century, Britain considered Russia to be her chief rival, and was monitoring the state of the Imperial Navy with great interest, amidst the fear that such rebellions might spread to the British presence in northern India. Worse, the British government realized that interior problems similar to Russia's existed in the homeland. Tsarist authorities attempted to keep the peace by issuing false reports, probably sent through the American consul, that all was well and that the crew and ship had already been captured. British reports from Odessa countermanded that story. Between the two countries, what passed for reliable news became "contradictory in the extreme."[68] It was the same American consul who remarked that Nicholas had by now "lost the affection of the Russian people,"[69] and publicly opined that the tsar "will never be safe [again] in the midst of his own people."[70] His perspective proved to be true in the long term.

Rather than attempt to elude the tsar's Black Squadron that arrived at Odessa, *Potemkin* went out to meet it with the intent of testing the resolve of the enemy's crews, and to sway them if

---

[64] Richard Cavendish
[65] Evan Andrews
[66] Richard Hough, The Potemkin Mutiny, Review by Victor P. Petrov, *The Slavic Review*, Vol. 21 No. 1, March 1962, p. 161
[67] Richard Hough
[68] Stefan-Catalin Trofin, The Mutiny on the Battleship Potemkin in the British Press – Europe Proceedings of Social & Behavioural Sciences – www.futureacademy.org.uk/files/images/upload/WLC2016FA127F.pdf
[69] History Learning Site, UK
[70] History Learning Site, UK

possible. Three battleships arrived in formation, including the *Tri Sviatitelia*, the *Dvenadsat Apostolov*, and the *Georgii Pobedonosets*. The *Tri Sviatitelia*, similar in dimensions and armory to the *Potemkin*, had been launched only a decade earlier, and served as flagship for the pursuit of the rebellious vessel. The *Dvenadsat Apostolov*, or *The Twelve Apostles*, was launched in 1890, and was older still. The Georgii Pobedonosets, the *St. George*, was likely the least effective of the three, as the fourth and final example of the older Ekaterina class warships. A second squadron arrived later in the morning with the *Rostislav* and the *Sinop* with the hope of capturing the *Potemkin* intact.

In a daring and unexpected confrontation, *Potemkin* made two passes through the middle of the tsar's formation, daring them to fire. The maneuver might have been utterly suicidal if the empathetic crew members aboard the Black Squadron vessels did not refuse to fire on fellow sailors. By now aware of what had happened at Tender Island, the tsar's officers may have developed a greater sense of caution in not pushing their orders too aggressively. The crew of the *St. George*, in fact, revolted in much the same way as the men of the *Potemkin* and "overran"[71] their officers, joining in with the revolutionary spirit. However, the urge to rebel hit a smaller minority on the *St. George*, and a loyalist counter-revolt returned the ship to the officers' control once they had sailed back into the harbor. The *Potemkin* threatened to fire on the *St. George* if she attempted to leave the harbor, and the ship was surrendered to the city garrison after her crew ran her aground. Seldom mentioned is that 45 of the sailors aboard the *St. George* refused to renew their vow to uphold their "oath of fidelity"[72] and were subsequently executed by firing squad.

When the loyalist ships turned away after *Potemkin* split their formation, Vice Admiral Aleksander Krieger, Acting Commander of the Black Sea Fleet, did his best to reason with the rebellious crew. Arguing at length, he failed to convince them to stand down in a conversation conducted via extensive flag signals. The mutineers sensed immediate victory once they were sure Krieger would not fire. Eventually, all Black Squadron ships were ordered back into Odessa harbor. Captain Kolands of the *Dvenadsat Apostolov* attempted to ram his own vessel into the *Potemkin*, with the intent of detonating his magazines at the same time. However, members of his crew thwarted the order, reversing engines and preventing officers from cutting detonation wires. Once in the harbor, the Black Squadron was occupied with double duty, keeping the peace and dealing with *Potemkin*, whose arrival gave the city's workers a new sense of confidence. Despite her inability to produce a fully committed revolution, a soviet of workers was established three months later as a result of the mutineers' efforts.

The End of the Mutiny

Potemkin put out to sea once more on the following day, leaving the tsar's ships in port as they

---

[71] Evan Andrews
[72] Russian Battleships.com

offered no pursuit. Unsure of what they had created in Odessa, the crew sailed west toward the Romanian port of Constanta, inspiring some minor actions along the way. Surrender was still not on the mutineer's minds, and Constanta represented a potential haven for food and fuel. Upon arrival, however, the *Potemkin*'s crew was shocked to be met with unexpectedly "strict formalities."[73] The Romanians offered nothing in the way of materials or asylum, until the ship was surrendered to authorities in the port. Their only armed protection, the crew of the *Potemkin* refused to give her up and departed the harbor for the town of Kefe, or Feodosia. More lightly defended than Odessa or Constanta, and perhaps more organized and empathetic, hopes for success in the Crimean port were high for a second uprising to further ignite the first.

The vast land holdings of Russia contain many ethnicities, and the Tatars of Crimea have little cultural connection with the European Russian populations of St. Petersburg or Moscow. The Tatars are Islamic and of Turkish heritage, which set Crimea at odds with the Russian Church of the Tsar, and later, the anti-religious structure of law in the Soviet Union. The predominant sect in Crimea objected to the term Tatar, as their language and affinities were Turkic. The Russian port of Sevastopol was not only located there for strategic reasons, but to preserve control over what had recently been a section of the Ottoman Empire. Catherine the Great had conquered it, after which she arrived soon thereafter with an entourage of 2,300 people to demonstrate that both she and Russia were safe there.

As the immediate aftermath of the mutiny made clear, 1905 was a timely one for the *Potemkin* incident. The Tatar population had undergone an awakening since the latter half of the 19th century, and was rapidly developing a "contemporary national consciousness."[74] With no love lost for Tsarist Russia, uprisings were common in almost every large Crimean community, based on a regional–more than national–world view. 1905 marked the beginning of a Tatar youth revolution that would bring sinister consequences decades later, with mass relocations in an attempt to diffuse the culture's strength.

The primary accounts of *Potemkin*'s attempt to procure supplies and fire up revolutionary fervor in Crimea differ. Upon the ship's arrival in Feodosia, the governing body of the city agreed to assist with provisions. The Russian military component, however, countermanded the local order, intervening to prevent any exchange of goods or political machinations between the *Potemkin* crew and dangerous social elements. Local revolutionaries who attempted to supply *Potemkin* were fired upon by the military. Although the crew's treatment spurred "large waves of protest," the situation did not reach the tipping point of unified rebellion. Some accounts claim that mutineers attempted to seize several barges carrying coal on the following morning. Ambushed by the port's garrison, 22 of the party's 30 members were either killed or captured. An alternate account suggests that *Potemkin* made no requests whatsoever of the town, only

---

[73] KCHF.RU, Battleship Kniaz Potemkin Tavrechevsky

[74] Hakan Kirimili, The 'Young Tatar" Movement in the Crimea, 1905-1909 – www.psi203.cankaya.edu.tr/uploads/files/Kirimili%20Young20%Tatar%20Movement20%in20%Crimea%201905-1909%20(1993)(2)pdf

demands. Representatives of the community met with the People's Committee on the ship, where they were threatened with mass bombardment if they did not provide "500 tons of coal, meat, lard, cattle and matches."[75] A third account claims that only two were killed in the raiding party, and that seven jumped overboard, to be saved later. A new wave of protests spread through Feodosia, the major port of Sevastopol, and in Akmescit, known in Russia as Simferopol. In that city, the *Potemkin*'s impetus caused a storming of the prisons in the following months, with more pogroms carried out against the Jewish population.

The ship's plight also helped to bring about the emergence of a revolutionary leader, Lieutenant Pyotr Schmidt, who was responsible for bringing about widespread protests which the *Potemkin* crew had initially anticipated. The Lieutenant Commander of *Destroyer Number 253* in the Black Sea Fleet enhanced the *Potemkin*'s fervor with a famous speech in Sevastopol, calling for a release of political prisoners and an observance of citizens' rights. As had Matyushenko aboard the *Potemkin*, Schmidt openly declared, "If we are not given universal suffrage, we shall once more proclaim the great all-Russian strike."[76] Schmidt was fortunate to end up leaving Russian service with only a dishonorable discharge.

---

[75] Russian Battleships.com
[76] Hakan Kirimli

Schmidt

Potemkin continued to issue declarations as well, with broadcasts of manifestos "to all civilized citizens and to the working people."[77] In an attempt to convince local sentiment that revolutionary progress was further along in other locales than it truly was, *Potemkin* described the entire nation as "burning with indignation."[78] Still, to expect the citizenry's rancor to spill over entirely was premature. The military did not buckle, and the duma ceded to Russian directives.

The *Potemkin*, by some accounts, left Feodosia empty-handed. However, the report of the *Potemkin*'s activities in the port as handed to Vladimir Lenin after the Soviet takeover more than a decade later differ somewhat. This account claims that *Potemkin*'s food stores were replenished in port, and that the crew successfully seized a Russian merchant ship carrying a full load of

---

[77] Marxist.org, V.I. Lenin, The Latest News Report – www.marxist.org/archive/lenin/works/1905/jul/10d.htm
[78] Marxist.org

cattle. A particular affront to the government, the victimized ship turned out to be the *Grand Duke Alexei*. Similarly, their coal reserves were at least in part restored through a transaction with a British ship. By that time, according to the Lenin report, there was still no thought of surrender, and the subsequent destination was still unknown. There is no tangible account of low morale among the crew, and the task of sparking revolution within the Black Sea remained the ship's primary mission.

Such confidence, however, was bound to erode over their 11-day tour of the Black Sea's coastline. When crew expectations went unmet by the population on shore, *Potemkin* set sail for one more visit to Constanta, reconsidering the Romanian offer of asylum in exchange for surrender of the ship. Romania had no particular use for *Potemkin*, and would certainly have thought twice about indirectly stealing a Russian warship. Likewise, they had no taste for a political conflict with Russia, to the point where offering asylum to the *Potemkin* crew was as much courage as they would dare to demonstrate. With few other options, Romania's terms of protection were accepted, and the ship was turned over to authorities in the port of Constanta. The crew of *Ismail* did not follow *Potemkin*'s course, returning to Sevastopol to surrender directly to the Russians, and to face a harsh military brand of justice.

Matyushenko, however, had one more statement to deliver to the tsar, and fed the engine sea water, leading to its breakdown. Before departing the ship, he opened all the Kingston valves and other seacocks throughout the vessel, allowing it to flood and sink to the bottom of the harbor. Once ashore, Matyushenko and the others declared themselves political refugees and requested protection. Despite the uprisings that would spring from the growing *Potemkin* legend through the following months, the ship's participation in the sputtering revolution simply "petered out."[79]

The surrender of *Potemkin* in Constanta, like the story of Feodosia, indicates that the rebel ship had not always been a good guest as it sought assistance and political converts. For Constanta, *Potemkin*'s arrival was the most "publicized event" of the year. Neither the Romanian authorities nor the public had any idea as to *Potemkin*'s intentions when it arrived eight miles off the coast. The garrison was immediately alerted and an artillery battery was quickly established, but Constanta knew it could not effectively oppose the battleship. *Potemkin* eventually anchored less than two miles outside the harbor. Three decidedly inferior vessels were sent out to defend the city, with the artillery at their backs. Part of the *Psezuape*'s crew expressed a desire to join the *Potemkin* crew in rebellion, but such a move was dissuaded. Among the public, her arrival caused what one observer called a "living unrest," despite Matyushenko's reassurances that *Potemkin*'s mission was to resist the autocracy, rather than to slaughter innocent civilians.

The Ministry of War started the first round of talks with the mutineers, offering a guarantee against extradition to Russia if the crew laid down its weapons and vacated the ship. Tensions reportedly "peaked" around 4:35 in the morning the following day when *Potemkin* turned to port,

---

[79] Richard Cavendish

and the Romanian vessel *Flag* prepared herself to fire. *Potemkin* left the harbor, not to return until June 25.

On the second visit, the crew was far more willing to discuss surrender of the ship for asylum. Romanian Commander Nicolae Negru oversaw the *Potemkin* as it relocated to shore. Two hours later, the *Potemkin* crew was at stations and in the presence of the public, "assisting with satisfaction at the end of this event."[80] According to Negru's written account, some of which is tensely humorous, he describes the shot fired by *Potemkin* when greeting Romanian forces. Misunderstanding the gesture, his military clerk 'turned pale."[81] Negru went out to meet *Potemkin* aboard the *Flag*, which Romanians jokingly referred to as "a poor boat with a pair of shovels."[82] Negru forced the clerk to accompany him, but the underling complained the same thing would happen as had taken place at Tender Island, and that he had a wife and children. As the only one among the party to speak coherent Russian, he had no choice.

Soon after their arrival on the *Potemkin*, Sergeant Matyushenko appeared with his committee. Negru greeted him, and explained that his presence was intended as nothing more than a courtesy extended to all visitors. In the minutes that followed, Matyushenko suddenly drew his revolver before the commander, who took two steps back. The terrified pilot of the *Flag* did not understand Matyushenko had been relating the story of how he had killed officers at Tender Island. Negru calmly urged Matyushenko to put the weapon down, and the unpredictable revolutionary, believing that the Romanian liked the gun, offered it freely to him. Negru asked the mutineer how long he would like to stay in Romania, and what his needs might be. Matyushenko provided no answer for the duration of the crew's intended stay, but explained that the men required food and pay. When Negru expressed a reluctance to supply those needs based on his lack of authority, Matyushenko stiffened and threatened to bombard the city, after which the Romanian promised to consult with his superiors at once.

The second round of talks was personally overseen by Romanian Prime Minister Gheorghe Grigore Cantacuzino. Once the agenda had been settled between the parties, the crew erupted in a fit of joy and relief. As they prepared to exit *Potemkin*, lockers were broken open, and whatever manner of equipment that could be carried was taken. Sailors were greeted on shore by a crowd thought to number more than 8,000. Dancing between sailors and citizens was rampant, and many seamen gave their berets and ribbons to the crowd as souvenirs. Despite Romania's guarantee that the sailors were free to go wherever they wanted, some held no trust in the agreement, believing they would soon be arrested, extradited, or executed. One enclave was housed in Anadalchoi, a hamlet near Constanta. Of the sailors, only six went abroad. Matyushenko was personally received by Prime Minister Cantacuzino. Two officers and a mechanic received personal invitations from the royal family at Sinaia. The offer of political

---

[80] Richard Cavendish
[81] Trofin
[82] Trofin

protection finally came from Romania's King Carol I, known in the West as Charles I. All the sailors knew was that, in the first days, that they had traded in bad borscht for Romanian prioski, fried buns, eaten with a variety of fillings.

Gheorghe Grigore Cantacuzino

Following the 11-day drama that initially appeared as though it might overthrow the tsarist system ruling the largest land mass on earth, the *Potemkin*'s crew slipped silently away through Constanta, then went on their separate ways. Having tasted Russian naval discipline firsthand, returning to Russia was not a pleasant notion, although some did come back with the full knowledge of what would likely happen to them. The *Potemkin* was refloated, and a few original crew members assisted in her return to the port at Sevastopol as part of a "special crew."[83] She was returned to Russia the following day. Romania required every sailor who stayed within the national borders to enlist in the military for the remainder of the time they would have spent in service to Russia. A few returned home to be summarily executed, though many more stayed abroad as political emigrants.

When the Russians arrived to retrieve *Potemkin*, matters did not begin smoothly, as she had

---

[83] Kchf.ru

been half sunk in the harbor and was flying the Romanian flag. Negru was treated coldly by the Russian Admiral for allowing the criminal crew to escape onto shore, but by the second day, all that seemed to have changed. Following a lengthy conversation on all manner of topics, some entirely unrelated, the Admiral ended the proceedings by declaring, "But enough of all this. Let's drink a cup, and then tell dirty anecdotes!"[84] Some face was lost when the Russians first attempted to refloat *Potemkin*, flooded the bilge in error, and almost sunk the ship again.

The condition of the vessel was deplorable at best. Many of her windows had been broken, and spots of blood dotted the ship's decks. Mirrors and cabinets had been largely destroyed, and the infirmary more nearly resembled a slaughterhouse, exuding a "cadaverous odor"[85] throughout the ship.

As Russia came out of Tsushima with an entirely undeserved gift of political grace courtesy of the American president, so they did with the rebellion by reducing it to no more than a squabble over food. This time, the tsar had to arrange the *Deus ex Machina* without the help of the American presidency. Russia further improved its international image, pretending to scold Romania for releasing their crew, but secretly rewarding her for returning the ship and restraining any additional impetus toward supporting their neighbors' rebellions. Diplomatically, the affair was handled "tongue in cheek,"[86] and no new conflicts took hold as a result of the *Potemkin* affair.

The press reported incessantly on the entire *Potemkin* adventure as it impacted Constanta. Most reports flowed directly from whatever "political sympathies"[87] were held by the leadership of the newspaper. Some conducted their own investigations, and sensationalistic accounts were abundant, including depicting sailors breaking out in tears as they remembered events in Odessa. The affair caused trepidation among neighboring nations, and shaped immediate policy for similar rebellions. Bulgaria reacted immediately, requiring any insurgents along its territory be immediately disarmed and removed. The sultan forbade any of its ships to venture past the Black Sea for fear of onboard revolts. Even Romanian opinion was sharply divided, with many calling the granting of asylum a "violation of sovereignty."[88]

The Legacy of the *Potemkin*

In the following years, a few crewmen were "lured back to Russia by trick,"[89] then either exiled or executed. They were arrested and imprisoned awaiting sentence, regardless of their current passport status. A large percentage of the crew returned to Russia after the revolution 12

---

[84] Paul Dominte
[85] Paul Dominte
[86] Stefan-Catalin Trofin
[87] Paul Dominte
[88] Paul Dominte
[89] Robert W. Clawson, An American Businessman in the Soviet Union: The Reimer Report, The Business History Review, Vol. 50 No. 2 (Summer 1976) p203

years later. In the meanwhile, despite most others doing their best to maintain a low profile, Matyushenko became a "celebrity revolutionary"[90] who appeared in many locales over the next two years, still berating the tsarist government in public venues. Once on shore from the *Potemkin*, he was sheltered by the elderly revolutionary, Zamfir Ralli in Constanta. From there, he traveled on to Switzerland, where he personally met with the exiled Lenin, but was soon deported to Austria for his involvement with illegal political groups. After a brief period there, he found himself in New York City working at a Singer sewing machine factory, but the pull to return and personally take on the tsar was irresistible. In 1907, he returned by way of England, and then Paris before crossing into Russia once more. It was only a matter of time before he was arrested there. This most extreme revolutionary of all, so individualistic that he could "barely stand any of the other revolutionaries,"[91] including Lenin, was executed by hanging in 1907 in the Crimean city of Sevastopol. His final words were understandably defiant, and not without accuracy: "Hang me, you cowards, but the time will come when it will be you hanging from the lamp posts in the street."[92] The Soviet dossier on Matyushenko suggests he was a man irresistibly drawn to his enemy, and one who believed he would triumph regardless of the odds. He was the perfect representation of the man who "can't take it anymore,"[93] colliding with officers who were authorized to arrest and execute him. Nicholas, his nemesis, would not be deposed for another 10 years.

For all the partial rebellions caused by the *Potemkin* incident through the Schmidt uprisings in a period of a few months, most estimates place the number of sailors either killed in action or executed later at around 2,000. Jewish deaths in the pogroms following are estimated in the range of 3,000. In the end, the seminal mutiny of the *Potemkin* and those rebellions that came after were crushed by "betrayals, poor timing, and lack of support by those on land."[94]

The actions taken aboard the *Potemkin* may have reinforced Nicholas's hesitation to continue the Russo-Japanese War, as he realized that the "unquestioning loyalty"[95] of his military forces was no longer guaranteed. Nevertheless, enough loyalist sentiment remained in the land and sea forces to put down various rebellions with relative ease.

The question will always remain as to whether Matyushenko, as the ideological leader of his crew, might have enjoyed a more successful revolution if he had proceeded in a more strategic manner. Certainly, the combination of strikes, protest marches, abuse at the hands of federal troops, and humiliating military losses must have made the landscape appear as if all was in place. It is difficult to imagine how a gifted rhetorical hothead such as Matyushenko could have resisted it. The miscalculation allowed a scheduled and coordinated action to give way to a knee-

---

[90] Evan Andrews
[91] Neal Bascomb
[92] Libcom.org
[93] Neal Bascomb
[94] Neal Bascomb
[95] Military, Russian Battleship Potemkin – www.military.wikia.com/wiki/Russian_Battleship_Potemkin

jerk response, based on bad beef. There, too, the heat of the insult was difficult to resist, as the leap from poor treatment to diminished human status was not difficult to make. Mutiny, in itself, cast the die for those aboard the *Potemkin*, but in witnessing the chaos on the streets of Odessa, there was no apparent path for the revolution to go back either, whether or not it was prepared to succeed.

As an example to fellow revolutionaries and crews, *Potemkin* did not produce the collective reflex with the immediacy that had been expected, becoming a more powerful symbol of upheaval in the ensuing months and years, instead. The resulting reality of 1905, after all the hopes of reaching the tipping point, was that of a lone ship trapped in the Black Sea, low on food and coal, with nowhere to go. The weakness of that lone ship was its inability to find a source of resupply, as the only available ones were in dedicated ports controlled by its enemy. With no safe haven, *Potemkin* could only rebel for so long.

Its increased power years later, however, helped to materialize the "major insurrection"[96] that would push the tsar to reform, and eventually remove him from the throne. To the Soviet presence of post-revolution years, *Potemkin* resounded as the first example of a conscripted crew to overthrow a tyrannical federal authority. In this way, the 11-day failed adventure became part of the Soviet Union's "founding mythology."[97] Some historians are surprised by the low profile sought by ex-crew members who disappeared into Romania and other countries. Outside of the human interest aspect, such as the sailor who settled in London, opened a restaurant, and lived to be well over 100 years of age, no individuals continued an overt campaign for a continued revolution.

Reforms on the part of Nicholas's government did occur in the form of concessions to the constitutionalist cross-section of the nation. Enough conciliatory gestures were offered and enacted to stall the impetus of outright revolution, and a 1905 constitution was hastily assembled, overflowing with superlatives for a non-aristocratic agenda. In the rare case of making good use of a political opportunity, Nicholas's new document declared proudly that "man, his rights and freedom are the supreme value."[98] It boasted the promise of free elections and representation for the common man, with an added promise that a citizen of Russia could not be stripped of his citizenship. Due to the reality of Russian ethnic diversity over such a large land mass, the document took the obligatory step of protecting cultural and ideological diversity, while shying away from the mixing of the social and economic classes. The aristocracy, without a doubt, would remain the aristocracy. However, once the effects of these inauthentic appeasements calmed passions to the point where Nicholas felt once more secure, their salient points fell into neglect, prompting one historian to observe that "history is full of paper constitutions with little or no effect."[99]

---

[96] Bright Hub Engineering
[97] Bright Hub Engineering
[98] Richard Cavendish

While the furor of 1905 abated for a time, *Battleship Potemkin* began another term of service for the Tsar's Imperial Navy. In order to quickly erase her troubling history, she was given the new name of *Panteleimon*, or *Pantaleon*, after Saint Pantaleon. Her subsequent missions were colorful, if not always successful. In 1909, she accidentally sank a Russian submarine, and was badly damaged when she ran aground in 1911. The aging ship participated in the Battle of Cape Sarych, after Russia declared war on the Ottoman Empire. In November of 1914, *Pantaleon* joined a convoy of the Black Sea Fleet, including five "obsolete," [100]pre-dreadnought warships. A bombing of the Ottoman coast commenced, and one Turkish ship was destroyed. The *Pantaleon* survived. She was involved in the bombardments of Bosphorous fortifications through early 1915, and upon being attacked by the German battlecruiser, *SMS Goeben*, joined with other pre-dreadnoughts to drive her off. When the first dreadnoughts entered service in the same year, *Pantaleon*'s role became secondary, and she was reduced to reserve status in 1918. After the armistice was signed in November of that year, she was handed over to the allies. In the following year, her engines were destroyed by the British in the withdrawal from Seavastopol, to prevent it being used by advancing Bolsheviks against the White Russians. She was finally abandoned when the Whites evacuated Crimea in 1920, and scrapped by the Soviets in 1923. Much of the famous 1925 film on her Black Sea rebellion story was filmed aboard the *Dvenstadt Apostolis*, one of the battleships that had pursued her into Odessa harbor.

It is often observed that the *Potemkin* saga served as the dress rehearsal for the 1917 revolution that ended the tsarist government. One could say it served as one of two dress rehearsals, as the "spate of mutinies"[101] over the following months was an expansion of *Potemkin* inspiration. With so many participants, each requiring an agenda, goal, and good timing, *Potemkin* struck too early to bring together a struggling class of capitalists and workers, landlords and peasants, the masses as a whole, and a tsarist monarchy wielding "a powerful apparatus of oppression."[102] However, the development of a worker's soviet only a few months later served as a testament to the crew's efforts.

Lamentably, the tsar did not learn the lessons of 1905, and the presence of inedible food on the tables of Russian ships was cause for continued rebellions over the following seven years, causing death, injury, and numerous arrests. With World War I coming on the heels of the 1905 disturbance, Russia was unable to manage "rebuilding its morale"[103] before being required to fight again. Schmidt's many uprisings continued to drain Moscow's energies, involving 34 different ships, 12,000 sailors, and over 10,000 soldiers. Uprisings erupted even in Sevastopol, Russia's primary Crimean port. *Potemkin* even hastened the political engagement of the peasant

---

[99] Daron Acemoglu, Economic Origins of Dictatorship and Democracy, Review by Allen Deoyen, *The Economic Journal*, Vol. 117 No. 517 (Feb. 2007) p162

[100] Military

[101] Alpha History, The 1905 Revolution: Kerensky Overthrown; Peace is the Demand of the Maximalists – www.alphahistory.com/russianrevolution/1905-revolution

[102] Marxist.com

[103] Robert Zelowski, Lieutenant Peter Petrovich Schmidt, *Jahrbücher für Geschichte Osteuropas*, p29

class. The All-Russian Peasant Union met for the first time in Moscow, one month later. Their first resolutions called for nationalization of land without compensation, with the peasant committee as distributors. They called for universal suffrage, but rejected the idea of a democratic republic. Lenin's "democratic dictatorship of workers and peasants"[104] had taken a step toward the realization of the Bolshevik creed. The *Potemkin* crew represented one of the two constituents that formed the ideal for leadership, workers, and peasants. The All-Russian Peasant Union was, in Lenin's words, a group that was "unquestionably revolutionary at the bottom."[105]

The Soviet Union applied the *Potemkin* story not only as a chapter in its own glorious history of overcoming tyranny, but as a model for the overthrow of foreign governments as well, most notably the United States. Lenin considered *Potemkin*'s courageous act as an "initial step"[106] toward ultimate victory in 1917. He excused the lack of literal victory in *Potemkin*'s case, and he opted for employing it as a conceptual model instead, describing the ship as he would a plot of land as an "undefeated territory [and] the nucleus of a revolutionary army"[107] Likewise, the early leaders of the USSR "repackaged"[108] the Potemkin crew as heroes of the revolution, despite their early entry into the process. The idea of a rebellious militia became an honorable calling among the Soviets, and even Leon Trotsky, the Commissar of War, insisted there must be a fully armed citizenry. Soviet leadership hailed a group of uneducated serfs that overthrew the aristocracy and managed to operate a fully-armed battleship without the benefit of privileged officers.

---

[104] History Learning Site, UK
[105] History Learning Site, UK
[106] Military
[107] Russapedia, On This Day: Russian in a Click, 27 June – www.russipedia.com/on-this-day/june-27/
[108] Evan Andrews

Trotsky

For some, the *Potemkin* incident was just a "sordid little rebellion,"[109] but for the Soviet Union in the wake of the overthrow of Nicholas II, it was a defining and "glorious moment," justifying their belief in the superiority of the system.

Online Resources

Other Russian history titles by Charles River Editors

Other titles about the Potemkin on Amazon

---

[109] U.S. Naval Institute, The Potemkin Mutiny – www.usni.org/store/books/blue-jacket-books/potemkin_mutiny

Bibliography

HMS *Wager*

Anon. *An Affecting Narrative of the Unfortunate Voyage and Catastrophe of His Majesty's Ship Wager*. London: J. Norwood, 1751.

John Bulkley and John Cummins. *A Voyage to the South-Seas in the Years 1740-1*. London: Jacob Robinson, 1743. Second edition, with additions, London, 1757.

John Byron. *Narrative of the Hon. John Byron; Being an Account of the Shipwreck of The Wager; and the Subsequent Adventures of Her Crew*, 1768. Second edition, 1785.

Alexander Campbell. *The sequel to Bulkeley and Cummins's voyage to the South-seas*. London: W. Owen, 1747.

Isaac Morris. *Narrative of the Dangers and Distresses which befel Isaac Morris and seven more of the crew*. London: S. Birt, 1752.

Pack, S. W. C. (1964). *The Wager Mutiny.* A. Redman.

Somerville, Henry Boyle Townshend (1934). *Commodore Anson's Voyage into the South Seas and Around the World.* W. Heinemann.

HMS *Bounty*

Alexander, Caroline. *The Bounty: The True Story of the Mutiny on the Bounty*. Penguin Books. (2011)

Bligh, Captain William. *Mutiny on the Bounty.* Digireads.com. (2011)

Howard, Richard A (March 1953). "Captain Bligh and the Breadfruit". Scientific American: 88–94. Reprinted in Human Nutrition. "Readings from Scientific American" series (1978).

Morrison, James (1935). The journal of James Morrison, boatswain's mate of the Bounty, describing the mutiny & subsequent misfortunes of the mutineers, together with an account of the island of Tahiti. Golden Cockerel Press.

Nordoff, Charles and James Hall. *Mutiny on the Bounty.* Create Space Independent Publishing Platform (2014)

Toohey, John (1999). Captain Bligh's Portable Nightmare. Fourth Estate. ISBN 1841150770.

Walters, Stephen S., ed. The Voyage of the Bounty Launch: John Fryer's Narrative. London: Guildford, 1979, and various private and boutique publishers.

Young, Rosalind Amelia (1894; 2003). Mutiny of the Bounty and the story of Pitcairn Island: 1790–1894. University Press of the Pacific.

The *Amistad*

Jackson, Donald Dale (1997). "Mutiny on the Amistad". Smithsonian 28

Jones, Howard (1987). *Mutiny on the Amistad: The Saga of a Slave Revolt and Its Impact on American Abolition, Law, and Diplomacy*. New York: Oxford University Press.

Osagie, Iyunolu Folayan (2000). *The Amistad Revolt: Memory, Slavery, and the Politics of Identity in the United States and Sierra Leone*. Athens: University of Georgia Press.

Owens, William A. (1997). Black Mutiny: The Revolt on the Schooner Amistad,

Pesci, David (1997) Amistad, Da Capo Press

Rediker, Marcus. (2012). *The Amistad Rebellion: An Atlantic Odyssey of Slavery and Freedom*. New York: Viking.

Zeuske, Michael (2014). "Rethinking the Case of the Schooner Amistad: Contraband and Complicity after 1808/1820". Slavery & Abolition 35

Battleship Potemkin

Acemoglu, Daron, Economic Origins of Dictatorship and Democracy, Review by Allan Doeyen, The Economic Journal Vol. 117 No. 517 (February 2007)

Alpha History, The 1905 Revolution, Kerensky Overthrown; Peace is Demand of the Minimalists – www.alphahistory.com/russianrevolution/1905-revolution/

Andrews, Evan, The Mutiny on the Battleship Potemkin, History.com – www.history.com/news/mutiny-on-the-battleship-potemkin-110-years-ago

Abraham Archer, The Revolution of 1905: Russia in Disarray, Review by Scott J. Seregny, The Russian Review Vol. 48 No. 2 (April 1989)

Bascomb, Neal, Red Mutiny, Eleven Fateful Days on the Battleship Potemkin, May 27, 2007, Houghton Mifflin

Bright Hub Engineering, Russian Battleship Potemkin –
www.brighthubengineering.com/marine-history/124041-russian-battleship-potemkin/

Cavendish, Richard, The Mutiny on the Potemkin, History Today –
www.historytoday.com/richard-cavendish/mutiny-potemkin

Clawson, Robert W., An American Businessman in the Soviet Union: The Reiner Report, The Business History Review Vol. 50 No. 2 (Summer 1976)

Dominte, Paul, Study on the Battleship Potemkin – Its Impact on Daily Life –
www.anmb.ro.buletinstiintific/buletine/2011_Issue2/170-173.pdf

Encyclopaedia Britannica, Russo-Japanese War, 3-10-2008 –
www.britannica.comevent/Russo-Japanese-War

Encyclopaedia Britannica, Russian Revolution of 1905 – www.britannica.org/event/Russian-Revolution-of-1905

Flag.blackened.net, 1905 – www.flag.blackened.net-revolt/anarchism/winters.anarcho/history/1905.html

Food and Foodies in Japan, UCLA, Fall 2013 –
www.foodandfoodiesinjapan.wordpress.com/2012/02/29/battleship-potemkin-the-rebellion-for-food

Free Dictionary, All-Russian Peasant Union, Great Soviet Encyclopedia reprint –
www.encyclopedia2.freedictioinary.com/all-Russian+Peasant+Union

Great Soviet Encyclopedia, reprint Free Dictionary, Potemkin, 1979 –
www.encyclopedia2.freedictionary.com/Potemkin

Halpern, Paul G., The Mediterranean Naval Situation, Review by Daniel Horn, The Journal of Modern History Vol. 44, No. 2 (June, 1972)

Heyman, Neil M., Leon Trotsky's Military Education: From the Russo-Japanese War to 1917, The Journal of Modern History, Vol. 48 No. 2 (January 1976

KCHF, Battleship Kniaz Potemkin Tavrichevskiy – www.kchf.ru

Kirimli, Hakan, The Young Tatar Movement in Crimea 1905-1909, Cahiers du Monde Russe et Sovietique Vol. 34 No. 4 (Oct-Dec. 1993)

Libcom.org, Matiushenko Afasny Nikolaevich 1879-1907 –
www.libcom.org/history/matiushenko-afasny-nikolaevich-1879-1907

Marxist.com, In Defense of Marxism, Alfansy Matushenko, the Revolt on the Armoured Cruiser Potemkin – www.marxist.com/revolt-armoured-cruiser.htm

Marxist.org, V.I. Lenin, The Latest News Report – www.marxist.org/archive/lenin/works/1905/jul/10d.htm

Military, Russian Battleship Potemkin, Revolutionaries Had "No Care" for Communism – www.military.wikia.com/wiki/Russian_battleship_Potemkin

Odessasecrets, the 1905 Pogrom, Monday Archives June 15, The Battleship Potemkim Mutiny, 14 June 1905/27 June 1905 – 11-Years-On – www.odessasecrets.wordpress.com/2015/06/

Ralhmag.com, Neal Bascomb, Red Mutiny Reviewed – www.ralphmag.org/Fl/potemkin.html

Russapedia, On This Day, Russia in a Click, 27 June – www.russapedia.ru com/on-this-day/june-27/

Russian Battleships, 1905-07 – www.russianbattleships.com/home/newspaper-clips-1900-1914/1905-07-07

Russian Warrior.com, The Imperial Navy (1900-1913) – www.russianwarrior.com/STMainhtml?1905_History_Navy.htm&l

Slideplayer, Why Did Nicholas II Survive in 1905, but Not in 1917 – www.slideplayer.com/3966949

The Daily Best, Cossacks: The Cowboys of Crimea – www.thedailybeast.com/articles/2014/03/12/cossacks-the-cowboys-of-crimea.html

The Great Soviet Encyclopedia, reprint Free Dictionary, 1979 – www.encyclopedia2.freedictionary.com/Potemkin

Trofin, Stefan-Catalin, The Mutiny on the Russian Battleship Potemkin in the British Press – European Proceedings of Social & Behavioural Sciences – www.futureacademy.org.uk/files/images/upload/WLC2016FA127F.pdf

Trueman, C.N., The 1905 Russian Revolution, History Learning Site, UK – www.historylearningsite.co.uk/modern-world-history-1918-to-1980/russia-1900-to-1939/the-1905-russian-revolution

U.S. Naval Institute, The Potemkin Mutiny – www.usni.org/store/books/blue-jacket-books/potemkin-mutiny

Weinberg, Robert, The Revolution of 1905 in Odessa: Blood on the Steps, Review by Maureen Perrie, The Slavonic and East European Review Vol. 73 No 1 (January 1995)

Wildman, Allan K., The End of the Russian Imperial Army: The Old Army and the Soldiers' Revolt, Review by Norman Saul, Slavic Review, Vol. 40 No. 3 (Autumn, 1981)

Yeltsin, Boris, Presidential Library, Black Sea Fleet Opened in Sevastopol, Sept.26, 1869 – www.prlib.ru/en-us/Pages/Item.aspx?itemid=673

Zeloski, Robert, Lieutenant Peter Petrovich Schmidt, Jahrbücher für Gesichte Osteuropas

Free Books by Charles River Editors

We have brand new titles available for free most days of the week. To see which of our titles are currently free, click on this link.

Discounted Books by Charles River Editors

We have titles at a discount price of just 99 cents everyday. To see which of our titles are currently 99 cents, click on this link.

Printed in Poland
by Amazon Fulfillment
Poland Sp. z o.o., Wrocław